BOAT BURNING FOR BEGINNERS

SWAPPING OUR 9 TO 5'S FOR SUCCESSFUL SELF-EMPLOYMENT

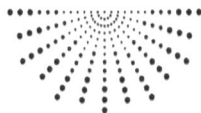

JESSICA CAMPOS   GERI DIVITA   MELINDA GARVEY

THERESA PORE   JENNIFER JOHNSON   SHELLEY LARSEN

JANNA PAULSON   JAMIE MATUSEK   ABIGAIL SEYMOUR

CONTENTS

ABOUT SULIT PRESS

Sulit Press is a boutique publishing house that provides high-touch support to thought leaders, industry shakers, and changemakers writing impactful nonfiction. Whether you're publishing a personal memoir, an industry-specific solo book, or contributing to a collaborative multi-author book, we help you go from aspiring author to published author—with clarity, confidence, and community.

Founder and CEO Michelle Savage is an international best-selling author, speaker, and mentor who helps high-vibe, heart-centered women share and amplify their stories. With a background in publishing, coaching, and storytelling, Michelle is passionate about helping women turn their lived experience into professional assets—whether that means a book, a brand, or a bigger platform.

She's led women through their first published pieces, hosted sold-out retreats, and built a thriving community of bold, generous authors who are ready to be seen.

Want to learn more? Visit www.sulitpress.com

INTRODUCTION

What does it *really* take to make the leap from a secure nine-to-five into entrepreneurship? To shake off the golden handcuffs, the illusion of safety, and go all in on building something of your own?

For many women, the risk feels too great. The dream of launching a business, creating something from scratch, is often overshadowed by fear.

How will I pay for health insurance? What about retirement? What if I fail?

But then there are the others; the ones who feel an ember inside. A flicker of desire to do things differently. To build something meaningful, with their name on the door. And instead of letting fear smother that ember, they fan it into flames.

These are the women who burn the boats.

No backup plan. No half-measures. Just a full-body yes to what could be, knowing there's no turning back. In the ashes of an old identity, a new one rises, entrepreneur, founder, leader.

When you run the show, you set the tone. You build the culture. You take off the professional mask and do business as yourself. You sell in your voice. You create something real—and that first sale? There's nothing like it!

But here's what most people won't say: building a business asks everything of you. You will work outside your comfort zone nearly every day. You'll grow in every direction—emotionally, spiritually, financially, and intellectually. You'll outperform your own limits, and yes, sometimes you'll fail. Publicly.

It's not for the faint of heart. It takes guts, grit, and a pinch of delusion. And for those who embrace it fully, it becomes something greater than just a job. It's a mission, a creative act and a test of resilience.

Entrepreneurs recognize each other by the scars and the stories. By the way they've weathered late nights, tight cash flow, client drama, supply chain chaos, and the lonely in-between moments where quitting looks easier than continuing.

And yet, they continue.

In this book, you'll read personal stories from women entrepreneurs across a range of industries. They've generously shared the truth behind the glossy headshots —the mindset shifts, the strategic pivots, the breakdowns and breakthroughs.

You'll hear from:

- A teenage mom who climbed the corporate ladder, built her skills, and eventually took the leap
- A woman diagnosed with a life-altering illness in the middle of a career pivot
- A former lawyer who built a new life in a new country, while learning English and launching a business
- A founder thriving in a male-dominated industry without compromising her power
- A high-achieving practitioner who hit burnout and rebuilt a more spacious, sustainable way of working

These are not stories of overnight success. They are stories of steady courage, of burning the old model to build something better.

Who this book is for:

- The woman sitting in a corner office wondering if she's meant for more

- The creative who's got the talent but needs the push to believe she can do it solo
- The founder in the early days who craves camaraderie and proof that she's not alone
- Anyone who's felt that ember flicker inside and is ready to fan it into flame

Inside these pages, you'll find inspiration, but also practical insight. Real talk about what it takes to move from idea to execution, from paycheck to profit. You'll hear what worked, what didn't, what nearly broke them, and what made it all worth it.

This is *Boat Burning for Beginners*. There's no map. Just fire, conviction, and a clear decision: you're not going back.

Let's go.

ALWAYS FORWARD, NEVER BACK

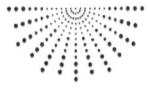

BY JESSICA CAMPOS

The cafeteria was where I finally snapped. It had been one week at this damn school, and I'd had enough.

I sat there, picking at my food while the girls at my table chatted about Disney vacations, beach houses, and which resort had the best pool. I had nothing to add.

I couldn't talk about riding Splash Mountain or dining with Cinderella. My childhood was a different movie. What was I gonna say?

That my dad was in prison? That I spent weekends in a visitation room, staring at plastic chairs and vending machines? The first time I visited, they told me it was a "hospital" so I wouldn't freak out.

Yeah. That would've been a real conversation killer.

One girl had a suitcase-sized cell phone because that's how it was before phones fit in your palm. Another was waiting for her father to pick her up in a private helicopter. Meanwhile, I was just hoping my mom could afford to send a public ride-share van to get me home. I had never felt so poor in my life.

So I just sat there, nodding, pretending, blood boiling, a movie playing in my head, every scene reminding me why I didn't belong there. In Spanish, we say: *una cucaracha en un balde de gallinas*. In English: a cockroach in a bucket of chickens about to eat you. That was me.

I felt awkward, out of place, like I had made a mistake coming here. Like I wasn't good enough. Like I wouldn't make it.

My friend Oliver was withdrawing from school. His mom was picking him up that afternoon. He said he was giving his spot to someone who would take advantage of the opportunity.

And I thought, *That's my sign. I'm doing the same thing.*

I walked toward the payphones, rehearsing the words in my head. I'd tell my mom I had made a mistake, that I didn't belong, that I should never have been accepted, and that someone else deserved my spot more. I had it all planned out, and I didn't even need coins. Someone had found a hack to bypass the payment: an extended code that made calls free.

One ring. Two. My mother answered.

"Pick me up," I said. No greeting. No small talk. "I don't want to be here. This was a mistake. Someone else should take my spot. I don't belong. I can't do this."

Silence.

Then, in the calmest, most direct voice I had ever heard, she said, "I hear you. We were told this would happen; that some of you would panic, feel out of place, and want to come home. But I'm not entertaining this, *mija*. What you start, you finish."

Click. She hung up.

I stood there, phone still pressed to my ear, my whole world tilting.

What the hell?

I was so pissed. That night, I poured every ounce of rage into a letter. I wrote about all the things she hadn't given me—how she was adopted, which meant my grandmother wasn't my grandmother. How I didn't even know my real family. How my dad was in jail. How she had made so many poor choices and left me with nothing.

I wrote so much that my middle finger had a dent from gripping the pen. When I finished, I folded the letter into thirds, licked the envelope, and slid it into my backpack, ready to mail it first thing in the morning.

Our dorm had eight girls. My bed was on the lower bunk, closest to the window. No air conditioning, just fans. At night, you could hear the *coquí* frogs singing outside, some distant radio playing from another room, and the occasional burst of laughter from down the hall.

I lay there, staring at the ceiling, furious. I had mapped my whole future around this place. This school was supposed to be my way out; my ticket to college, my independence, and a life beyond my hometown.

And now?

Tanto nadar para morir en la orilla. I swam and swam, only to die on the shore.

As I waited for my mother to reply to my letter, to say she'd changed her mind, to tell me she was coming to get me, I sat alone, stewing in my own frustration. I checked the mailroom every day. For a while, nothing. Then, a week later, a letter from my mom arrived. I tore it open, expecting...I don't know what. An apology? A promise that she was coming to get me?

Instead, she had written:

Jessica, you were given two arms and two legs. Do you know how fortunate you are?

I frowned. What the hell did that have to do with anything?

Some people are born with just one arm. Some can't speak and will never know what using their voice is like. Some survive accidents, their bodies covered in burns and scars they will carry for life. And you? You have a strong body. A voice that can be heard. A mind that can take you anywhere you want to go. You are exactly where you are supposed to be.

That was it. No sympathy. No softness. No lifeline. Just that.

I sat there, gripping the letter, feeling something in me crack open. I wanted to be angry. I wanted to write back and tell her she didn't get it.

But the truth was, she did.

Because what was my excuse? That these girls had more than me? That they talked about Disney while I spent weekends in a prison visitation room? So what? My mom was right. I still had two arms, two legs, and a brain. I still had a chance. And by then, I had taken a few quizzes and scored a couple of 100s. Maybe I could make it after all.

Looking back, my mom burned the boats for me. She made sure I had no way back. At the time, it felt harsh—even unfair. But now, I know it was a blessing. I didn't know it yet, but I was already learning how to handle pressure. That school I once hated gave me the foundation to keep going when life got hard; a foundation that would eventually carry me to law school, to entrepreneurship, and beyond.

Because what I learned is this: When you can't go back, you find a way forward.

Fast forward a few years to college, I believed that if I kept moving—kept checking the right boxes—I'd finally feel safe.

I got married to my middle school sweetheart, bought a home, became a mom, and I went straight from finishing my degree in business and marketing into law school.

I wanted to be a lawyer because I believed I could get my dad out of prison.

The irony? My dad was released.

I finished college, started law school, and took a job in the city far from my home in the south of Puerto Rico. That meant long, exhausting commutes—eighty-eight miles round trip every day.

Those drives became my second home. I spent hours in that car, stuck in traffic, stuck in my thoughts, stuck in a routine that felt endless. I kept a set of dumbbells in the car, doing arm workouts at red lights just to feel like I was making some kind of progress.

That commute wore me down. The distance, the exhaustion, the silence—it made me question everything. I remember thinking, *This can't be it. This can't be my life forever.*

Then one day, my husband told me he needed time. Time to think about our relationship.

"Time?" I thought. *You've known me since I was thirteen. What else is there to think about?*

But all I could picture were those commutes and the hours I spent driving to build a life I thought we both wanted. A life that wasn't working.

So I made a decision.

I told him he could keep the house. I couldn't carry the weight of those long commutes and an uncertain marriage.

I packed my things, found an apartment near my office, and moved out.

I didn't have time to grieve my marriage. I didn't have time to fall apart. I was too busy figuring out how to survive.

I became a single mom at twenty-four, balancing my job, raising my daughter, and trying to hold everything together. Mornings started before sunrise. I'd pack snacks and toys in the car, drop my daughter at daycare, then race to work. I'd spend the day juggling client meetings, endless paperwork, and trying to stay ahead in the foreclosures department—all while checking the clock, knowing that if I was even a few minutes late to daycare pickup, I'd be charged an extra fee.

Evenings were spent driving home in the dark, my daughter often falling asleep in the backseat before we even got inside. I'd carry her upstairs, microwave whatever dinner I could pull together, and collapse into bed only to wake up and do it all over again the next day.

There wasn't space to mourn what I had lost, no time to sit with the heartbreak. I just had to keep going. Work was going well—really well. I had built a solid reputation at the firm, managing nearly 300 active cases at a time. Efficiency was my superpower, and I turned my department into one of the firm's top-performing accounts. But no matter how good things looked on paper, there was one thing I couldn't ignore—my reality as a single mom.

I was chasing success, climbing the ladder, but I knew deep down that law firm life wasn't built for someone like me. Most nights, I'd leave the office and realize I was the only woman still there. Everyone else went home hours earlier. But the more time I spent there, the clearer it became: I couldn't keep living like this. I was exhausted, pouring everything I had into work, only to turn around and hand my entire paycheck to daycare. I was missing too much.

I knew I needed a change. Thankfully, a friend gave me some unexpected advice; that I could freelance for several law firms and actually make more money than I was at the firm. More importantly, I could control my own calendar.

I remember sitting down with a notebook, mapping out exactly how much I needed to earn. I calculate how many cases I needed each month just to stay afloat, and, if I hit my goal early, I'd take the afternoon off. Sometimes, if I had a good month, I'd spend a whole weekday at the beach, soaking in the freedom I'd finally found.

Freelancing wasn't just a new career move—it was my ticket to breathing room. A chance to heal. A chance to create something new. A chance to stop surviving and start living. A chance to own my calendar and be there for my baby girl.

For over a year, I kept my head down—no distractions, no chaos—just work and my daughter. Life finally felt steady. I had healed. I was done chasing things that didn't fit.

Then I met Tom; the American guy who would change everything.

I always joke that we met in bed, and well, kind of literally...but it's not what you think. It was a rooftop bar; one of those trendy spots with oversized leather beds instead of lounge chairs. Exhausted after a long week at work, I showed up still in heels with my blazer draped over my arm, planning to have one drink and go home.

And bam!

I noticed him, tall, clean-cut, and clearly not a local. With those blue eyes, I figured he was a tourist. So, I said hi. Turns out, Tom had been living on the island for over two years. He planned to work on Wall Street, but when things didn't pan out, his dad convinced him to move to Puerto Rico and help with the family's car dealership.

I don't remember what song was playing, but I remember feeling lighter than I had in months. For once, I wasn't the tired single mom juggling bills and court deadlines, I was just me again.

Tom fell in love with Puerto Rico; the food, the beaches, the rhythm of life. And when I met him, I swear he knew more about the island than I did. But what sealed the deal for me wasn't any of that. It was how he was with my daughter.

We quickly became a family of three. Got engaged. Planned a wedding. His business didn't survive, but we took the whatever-it-takes approach to keep things afloat. He applied for jobs. I sent him side hustle work from my office, and eventually, we landed an opportunity to open a property management company.

Little did we know, the mortgage crisis was about to change everything. The economy crashed, and my once-thriving law firm was drowning in overhead. I had two choices: cut expenses or abandon ship. So I cut myself. I took a temporary job two thousand miles away.

I told myself it was just for a few months. I rented an apartment, packed my bags, and promised to return soon.

I never went back.

I left the island with four suitcases and a Barbie castle for my little girl, a Puerto Rican woman, once terrified to leave home, now burning the boats with no way to return. Only thing? Those boats carried more than just my past. They carried my law degrees, my identity, and my dream of a beach house where I'd fall asleep to the sound of waves. They carried the chapters I thought defined me—a divorce, five years as a single mother, and a law firm built from nothing to millions.

I had spent my whole life chasing something, thinking law would save my dad, thinking family would heal my childhood wounds, thinking success would finally make me feel safe. But the moment I stepped onto that plane I knew none of those things were my destination. They were just the fuel that got me here.

Tom and I left Puerto Rico together. Starting over in Connecticut was overwhelming, but we were determined to make it work.

I took a temp job as an in-house counselor at a commercial real estate firm. At first, I was just another lawyer in a sea of attorneys auditing contracts. I kept my head down, did my work, and tried to keep my emotions in check.

I wasn't exactly sure what I wanted anymore, but I knew what I didn't want. I didn't want a career with a ceiling. I didn't want to feel boxed in. And I especially didn't want another divorce.

I was determined to build something stable that felt right for me, for Tom, and for our daughter.

Then, shortly after we moved, we found out we were pregnant. It wasn't planned, and honestly, the timing couldn't have felt worse. We were still adjusting to a new state, new routines, and new financial pressures. The excitement was there, but so was the anxiety.

I accepted a permanent role at the firm, grateful for the stability. On paper it seemed like a win, a steady paycheck, reliable hours, and a role that seemed secure. But deep down, I knew I couldn't stay there forever. I wasn't fulfilled. I wasn't growing.

Then, life gave me an unexpected push. While I was on maternity leave, my employer called. They weren't just cutting costs, they were cutting me.

I remember staring at the phone in disbelief. My stomach knotted with fear, but at the same time, something else stirred, relief.

Because that was the golden ticket.

The severance package gave me something I hadn't felt in years, freedom. No chasing clients, no exhausting commutes, no scrambling to survive. For the first time, I could pause and ask myself: *What now?*

One random Saturday morning, I saw it, an infomercial. A guy with abs of steel shouting: "This is P90X! Extreme Home Fitness! Are YOU ready to get in the best shape of your life?" I almost kept scrolling, but something hooked me. I grabbed my credit card and ordered it.

I made a deal with myself: I'll try it for ninety days. If it doesn't work, I'll send it back. But ninety days later? I didn't return it. Because something had shifted. For the first time since leaving Puerto Rico, I felt strong, physically, mentally, and emotionally. But more that, I felt in control.

It wasn't just the workouts, it was the discipline. No matter how tired or overwhelmed I felt, I hit play, and I followed through.

I started sharing my progress on Facebook, not to impress anyone, but because I was craving connection. I didn't have friends in Connecticut, and Tom's brutal commute left me alone most days. Posting online gave me a place to belong, and people noticed. They saw my progress, my consistency, my commitment. And soon, they started asking, What are you doing? Can you teach me?

Without even realizing it, I was a coach. I never set out to be a coach, influencer, or fitness expert. At first, I was just a woman trying to get her sh*t together. Every day, I showed up. Every day, I pressed play. Every day, I proved to myself I could do this.

And before I knew it, people were watching. Friends. Family. Strangers on Facebook. Then one day, I got the call. The company behind P90X was expanding, but they had yet to tap into one key market: the Hispanic market. They needed someone who understood the culture, the language, and the barriers. Someone with a real story. Someone who had walked the walk.

That someone was me.

I wasn't just coaching fitness. I was showing people what was possible — that you don't need privilege to create success, that you don't need a perfect past to build a future, that someone like *us*—a Latina, raised by a single mom, a woman who had to hustle for every opportunity —could lead the way.

And that? That changed everything.

As I poured my energy into coaching, I realized I was doing more than sharing workouts, I was building a community. An online one.

I got familiar with the idea of coaching online, organizing fitness classes on Zoom, sharing meal ideas, and helping people create healthier routines from the comfort of their homes. It wasn't just about fitness—it was about connection. And when you're immersed in changing lives like that, something shifts.

For me, that shift started to redefine my career. The more I invested in coaching, the more I realized I was stepping away from my identity as a lawyer and into something new, a wellness marketer.

During those early stages of building my coaching business, Tom and I got some unexpected news; I was pregnant with Baby Isabella. To be honest, I had lost so much weight that my period had become irregular. I ignored the signs for weeks, chalking it up to exhaustion. But one day, mid-push-up, I felt completely wiped out. Something felt...off.

When I finally went to the doctor, I was already fourteen weeks along.

The healthiest pregnancy I ever had.

Bella was two years old when Tom and I made the decision to move. The more I felt the fire from Tom's brutal work schedule, the clearer it became; I needed to replace his income so he could leave finance and join me. He had always wanted to be an entrepreneur, and when my side hustle hit six figures, we knew it was time.

We were going all in.

We Googled: *Best cities to raise a family in the U.S.* and Austin, Texas topped the list.

We had friends in Dallas and Houston, so we booked a trip. It was February, Connecticut winter, freezing, gray, and miserable. Austin? Paradise.

And then life threw another surprise.

During the trip, I realized I was late. I ran into a Walgreens, grabbed a pregnancy test, and took it in the bathroom. Two lines. Positive. Baby #4.

I didn't tell Tom right away. I waited until we were at The Oasis, overlooking Lake Travis. They offered margaritas. I passed. Tom gave me *the look.*

"What's going on?"

I slid him the test. His response?

"I guess we're officially moving to Austin. We can't fit in our house anymore!"

And just like that, we burned the boats. Again.

Moving to Austin made perfect sense.

Our Connecticut home had lost value, and financially, we were in a rough place. Between my condo in San Juan and our home in Trumbull, CT, both sitting underwater, we had accumulated $300,000 in debt.

We considered bankruptcy. But when we saw how much momentum my wellness business was gaining, we realized building income was our best way forward.

Have you ever seen those ads where people claim they made $75,000 in a weekend? That could've been our story, except we weren't flashy about it.

Our business took off faster than we imagined. Selling a $129 product turned into a powerful mix of affiliate commissions and bonuses for leading the Hispanic market expansion, giving us the runway we needed to move to Austin and start fresh.

But even with that success, we had to adjust. Tom returned to work for stable income and health insurance while I kept building the wellness coaching business.

We downsized, stuck to a tight budget, and stayed disciplined. There were no shortcuts, just consistent effort.

Tom balanced his full-time job with two side hustles; one helping his dad and another supporting my fitness business. Meanwhile, I immersed myself in learning. I joined marketing programs, studied personal development, and soaked up knowledge wherever I could.

I deeply believed the more you become, the more you'll earn.

I trained with mentors like Brendon Burchard and John Maxwell, and what began as fitness coaching evolved into something far bigger, something sustainable, meaningful, and truly ours.

Looking back, there's one thing I regret. It took me nine years to speak English fluently. And even when I moved to Austin, I kept myself in a bubble. I coached in Spanish, stayed in my comfort zone, and avoided stepping into unfamiliar spaces. A few years in, I still hadn't connected with many people outside my Spanish-speaking circle.

At one point, I told Tom, "Maybe I should just go back home."

"You haven't given my people a chance," he said.

And he was right. I spent years building a life in Austin with one foot still in the familiar. I was playing small, waiting for success to happen on my terms. But success doesn't work that way. You have to meet opportunity where it lives.

So, I pushed myself to show up differently. Three years into Austin, I attended a women's networking event; no safety net of Spanish, no hiding in familiar circles. Just me, showing up fully. That event changed everything.

For the first time, I connected with women building businesses, making an impact, and supporting each other in ways I hadn't experienced before. It opened my eyes— I had been boxing myself in, holding back because I was afraid to step into unfamiliar spaces.

I decided to keep showing up. I introduced myself to strangers, joined local events, and shared what I knew, no agenda, no sales pitch, just a genuine desire to connect. That's when I realized that people didn't just need information. They needed community. They needed a space where they felt seen, supported, and connected.

That's why we launched heyATX, a community built to serve business owners in Austin. But heyATX wasn't just about networking, it was about relationships. I knew how lonely it felt to build a business without a sense of belonging, and I wanted to create a space where people could feel supported no matter where they were in their journey.

At first, I leaned into what I knew best; coaching. I started by helping local entrepreneurs improve their social media presence, showing them simple, consistent ways to connect with their audience and build trust. People noticed.

Business owners began asking me to go beyond coaching. They wanted me to manage their social media for them. Before long, my side hustle had evolved into a done-for-you service. But I quickly realized social media alone wasn't enough. Entrepreneurs needed better websites, stronger messaging, and smarter marketing strategies to grow in a meaningful way.

That's when Tom joined me. While I handled content creation and strategy, Tom brought his operations skills to the table. Together, we turned my side hustle into a thriving business—expanding from social media management into a full marketing stack.

We launched ImpactLine Digital to help small businesses not just post content, but build real connections. Because visibility alone doesn't build a business, connection does.

Our agency grew quickly, and soon we found ourselves working with a wide range of clients. I've seen businesses go from $300,000 to three million dollars in revenue under my guidance. I've helped entrepreneurs bring their visions to life, including one client who went from an idea on paper to landing a show with National Geographic.

But as we grew, Tom and I realized something important. We wanted more than just growth. We wanted to build a business that aligned with our values.

That's when we decided to focus on wellness businesses, brands that aligned with our passion for health, longevity, and conscious living. With Tom's background as an ultra-marathoner, conversations about recovery, biohacking, and sustainable health practices were already part of our daily lives. Shifting our business to support wellness brands made sense both personally and professionally.

At ImpactLine Digital, our values guide every decision:

- People first, profits second- because meaningful connections always drive better results.
- Family- because building a business shouldn't cost you the people you love most.
- Transparency and authenticity- because honesty, even when uncomfortable, builds trust.
- Sustainability and consciousness- because the businesses that thrive are those that make a lasting impact.

Those values shape how we operate. If a client asks us to run manipulative or aggressive campaigns, we say no. If a strategy doesn't align with their mission, we advise against it, even if it means turning down an easy win. For us, success isn't just about revenue; it's about building something that lasts.

I used to believe success meant chasing; chasing degrees, promotions, achievements, and security. But chasing is exhausting. True success isn't about running after things. It's about aligning.

Aligning your work with your values. Aligning your goals with your strengths. Aligning your life with what matters most.

When Tom and I built ImpactLine Digital, we committed to those values—and because we stayed true to what mattered most, we've built a thriving agency that's helped brands generate over twenty million dollars in revenue.

And yet, despite all the wins, there are still moments when I feel like that girl sitting in the cafeteria, out of place and unsure if I belong.

Each time I step into boardrooms with investors and equity holders, Jessica—the girl with the cafeteria tantrum—tries to come back.

I hear that voice whispering: *You don't have corporate experience. You speak with an accent. You'll misspell words. They won't take you seriously.*

But then I remind myself of what I do have: A track record of generating over twenty million dollars in revenue. Proven strategies that deliver results. A business built from scratch, side by side with Tom, that continues to grow and thrive.

From a teenage girl waiting by the payphones, ready to give up on herself, to a woman who has built a beautiful life by overcoming one challenge at a time. I am living proof that we are powerful creators of our lives.

I didn't always know what the path would look like. Every major shift—giving love a chance after heartbreak, leaving my island to start over, stepping away from the law industry I worked so hard to build—started with nothing more than a gut feeling.

I couldn't predict how things would unfold, but I trusted that if I kept showing up, if I aligned my actions with what felt right, I'd find my way.

And I did.

JESSICA CAMPOS

Jessica Campos is proof that resilience and purpose can turn any challenge into an opportunity for transformation. When the 2008 mortgage crisis disrupted her successful law practice in Puerto Rico, she faced a crossroads. Instead of giving up, Jessica reinvented herself, transitioning into the wellness and digital marketing industries with the same tenacity and precision she brought to the courtroom.

Her bold pivot allowed her to build thriving communities and spearhead multi-million-dollar product launches, all while raising four children. Today, she works alongside her husband, Tom, combining their talents and passions to create a business that aligns with their shared purpose: empowering others to achieve their best.

Jessica's unique forensic marketing approach, informed by her legal and financial expertise, has made her one of the most sought-after digital marketers in the US. Named a Top 10 Digital Marketer and a recognized community leader, Jessica has helped hundreds of brands grow internationally, uniting people and driving meaningful change.

As co-host of HeyATX, Austin's fastest-growing networking community, Jessica continues to inspire connection and collaboration among professionals. Her accolades include being named one of Austin's Women to Watch, a Changemaker, and recipient of the Top Service Firm of the Year award.

When she's not revolutionizing brands, Jessica enjoys Austin's vibrant culture with her family, embracing the balance of work, wellness, and play. Her journey is a testament to reinvention, showing others how to transform challenges into opportunities and build a life of purpose and impact.

Learn more about Jessica's work here: www.impactlinedigital.com
Instagram: @jessicacamposofficial
LinkedIn: jessicamcampos

2

NEVER TOO LATE

BY GERI DIVITA

*J*t was a Saturday morning and I sat in my home office surrounded by a stack of bills, my heart heavy as I stared at the numbers. The calculations were simple, yet they carried an unbearable weight. Were we any closer to reaching our financial goals? Could I retire in 2022 as planned? I glanced at the oversized Post-It stuck to the back of my office door, where I had written my goals in 2018. Under the work section, I had boldly declared: *"Retirement: 3-31-22."*

The date loomed over me like a silent judge. My stomach dropped as I faced the truth—I wouldn't retire in eighteen months. The numbers didn't lie. A cold wave of disappointment swept over me. Two more years of grinding, sacrificing, pushing through exhaustion, and dealing with workplace politics. The thought felt like a dagger to the heart.

Outside, the scent of freshly cut grass and blooming flowers drifted through the window. My husband was out back, tending to the yard. When he came in and saw my tear-filled eyes, he knew something was wrong. As he wrapped his arms around me, I whispered the truth: "I'm not going to make it. I can't retire."

He listened intently, his steady presence grounding me. We both knew we had to take action. Failure was not an option.

I never expected my life to be easy, but I also never imagined the path I would take. At fifteen, I was supposed to be preparing for college, dreaming of independence. Instead, I was preparing for motherhood. A teenage pregnancy made me a statistic—the girl whose life was supposedly over before it had begun.

I married the father of my child because it felt like the right thing to do. He worked while I stayed home, and I was utterly dependent on him. I hated it. The feeling of having no control over my life gnawed at me. His mother taught me to drive, and I enrolled in vocational school with that newfound independence. Soon, I landed my first job in Accounts Payable, earning $600 a month.

From that moment on, I became a sponge. I learned everything I could, moving up the corporate ladder, but I always faced the same challenge: I wasn't college-educated. Determined to break that barrier, I enrolled in community college and worked tirelessly to prove myself.

Yet, despite my professional growth, my personal life was unraveling. We had a second child together, my beautiful daughter, but it wasn't enough to save us. The uneasy feeling about my husband's infidelity became unbearable. When I asked myself if I could stay in this marriage for the next five, ten, or twenty years, the answer was always "no." After ten years, we divorced.

Among my husband's friends was a man named David. I always admired his kindness and big heart. After my separation, I reached out to him. When he finally returned my call, he confessed that he had avoided me because I was married. Now, he was free to tell me how he truly felt.

I fell for him, fast and hard. Eighteen months later, we were married.

We built a life together, but I never stopped pushing myself professionally. In my thirties, a Vice President pulled me aside and offered me a chance to join a new division. I jumped at the opportunity. As part of a small but dynamic team, I wore multiple hats—operations, product management, sales, and marketing. I thrived in the fast-paced environment, but it came at a cost.

Then, my life took a devastating turn.

"There's been an accident," the voice on the other end said. I was told my son's uncle was taken to the hospital. But they didn't say anything about my son.

My stomach clenched, but I told myself it couldn't be that bad. My son was with his friends, heading to the family ranch. His father was meeting them there later that evening. Surely, I would have been told if something had happened to him.

But as the minutes stretched into hours, a deep unease settled over me. I checked my phone repeatedly, waiting for a message or a call—anything to confirm that he was okay. But the silence became unbearable.

Then the phone rang. I answered it, and my fingers suddenly became ice cold.

"This is the Sheriff from Jackson County," the voice said. "Ma'am, I need you to come to the coroner's office." A pause. "We need you to identify your son."

The words sent a shockwave through me, and I went numb. My body refused to move, to accept what I had just heard. The room blurred, the walls closing in.

This wasn't real. It couldn't be.

The drive to the coroner's office was two hours, but it felt like an eternity. My husband drove my ex-husband and me, his grip tight on the wheel, the weight of what lay ahead pressing down on us all.

I wanted to scream, to fight, to force the universe to undo this. But I could only nod numbly at the coroner's, confirming what they already knew.

It was him.

He was gone.

Grief is not a straight line. It does not follow logic or reason. It sneaks up on you when you least expect it— standing in the grocery store, waking up in the morning, hearing a song on the radio.

It was unbearable, and so I buried it. I threw myself into my work with a relentless, almost destructive force. I wouldn't have to feel if I stayed busy and kept moving. I could be numb.

I traveled three weeks out of the month, jumping from city to city; taking meetings, making deals, and chasing deadlines. My career became my identity, my armor. At work, I was competent. I was in control.

At home, I was a shell.

People told me to take time off—to grieve. But grief felt like a black hole, one I couldn't afford to fall into. So I didn't. I smiled when I needed to. I nodded when people offered condolences. And then I went back to work. It was my safe place.

Until the day my husband sat me down, his voice gentle but firm. "Your daughter needs you," he said.

I blinked at him, disoriented. "I'm here," I said, even though we both knew that wasn't true.

"No," he said, shaking his head. "She's growing up, and she's struggling. She needs her mother."

Something inside me cracked. I had lost one child. And now, without realizing it, I was losing another. She was only twelve, and she needed me.

Tears blurred my vision. I looked around the house—at the suitcase sitting half-packed by the door, the stack of unopened mail, and the empty dinner table. My work had become my escape, my lifeline. But my family, my daughter, was here. And she was slipping through my fingers.

I had to make a choice. And this time, I chose her. I chose us.

And so, I decided to step away. It wasn't easy. Walking away from the identity I had built, the safety of routine, felt like stepping off a cliff. But deep down, I knew—I had been running for too long. It was time to come home.

I had spent my whole life in California—the beaches, the weather, the energy. It was home. So when a recruiter called with a job opportunity in Texas, I laughed.

"Why would I move to Texas?" I scoffed at the idea to

my friend. "This California girl isn't leaving the best place on earth."

And yet, the thought lingered. The opportunity was good. It was tempting. But Texas?

The idea seemed absurd, until my husband, always the practical one, said, "Let's just go check it out."

A few weeks later we landed in Austin, and to my surprise, something shifted. The city had a different rhythm, one I hadn't expected. People made eye contact. Strangers held doors open. Kids addressed adults with "Yes, ma'am" and "No, sir," something I had never seen back home. It wasn't just a place; it was a culture—one of kindness, of warmth, of community.

We made the decision. Texas would be our new home.

The transition, however, wasn't simple. I started my new job first while my husband stayed behind in California to sell the house. We were building a custom home in Austin, a dream unfolding before us. Everything felt like it was falling into place. Until three months later when the General Manager resigned. Panic crept in. I had uprooted my life and moved across the country, and now my boss, my friend, the one who had hired me, the one I trusted, was gone. What did that mean for me? Would I be next?

I had options. The house in California hadn't sold yet. I could go back, but I didn't want to. I had fallen in love with Texas; more importantly, I wasn't ready to give up. Instead of panicking, I did what I did best—I looked for solutions. I started identifying gaps in the company, ways to improve processes, and places where leadership was needed. I took on extra responsibilities and made myself indispensable. It wasn't long before my efforts were noticed.

A few months later, I was promoted to Director, leading a team of over fifty people. The learning curve was steep, but I thrived. I implemented systems and streamlined operations and eventually transitioned into an IT role—something I had never envisioned for myself. The challenge was exhilarating. I wasn't just growing in my career but expanding my skill set in ways I had never expected. I had once thought Texas was an impossible move. Now, I couldn't imagine being anywhere else. What had started as a reluctant decision had become one of the best choices I had ever made.

On the surface, life was good. We had built a stunning custom home on a golf course, drove new cars, owned a boat, and spent weekends at the lake. It looked like a picture of success. But beneath it all, I felt something gnawing at me—a quiet, persistent discomfort that I couldn't shake.

Then, one day, as I stood in the middle of our oversized house, I had a moment of stark realization. Why did we build such a big house on a golf course when neither of us played golf?

I walked from room to room, staring at the rarely used spaces, feeling the weight of it all pressing down on me. The house had been a statement, a symbol that we "made it." But in reality, we were drowning. Our debt had grown as quickly as our salaries, and we had spent without a second thought. If we could afford it, we bought it.

The bills piled up, and the numbers became impossible to ignore. I started asking myself questions I had avoided for too long. How would we ever afford to retire? The lifestyle we had created wasn't sustainable, and for the first time, I saw it clearly. It was time to change. We put the house on the market and started looking for property. While our friends urged us to look west—where the prestige and price tags were higher—I knew in my gut that we would only end up in the same cycle again, so we did the opposite.

We looked east. And that's where we found it, an eight-acre parcel of land, raw and beautiful. It wasn't what I had envisioned initially, but something about it felt right. We had little money to spare, but my problem-solving skills kicked in. The seller agreed to finance, allowing us to purchase the land with little money down.

The hard part was breaking old habits. I started looking at custom home builders again, slipping into the familiar mindset of designing something grand. But my husband, ever the voice of reason, stopped me.

"Let's look at manufactured homes," he suggested. "They're taxed as personal property, so our taxes won't keep climbing." I stared at him, stunned. A manufactured home? It wasn't what I had pictured for us. What would our friends think? Our colleagues? Everyone we knew had custom-built homes. Could I do this?

And then it hit me. Ego. That same ego led us to buy the golf course home, the new cars, the boat, and the weekends on the lake. The same ego that whispered that success looked a certain way and anything else was a failure.

I forced myself to step back and really consider what we needed, not what looked good on paper or impressed others, but what truly made sense for our future.

We found a 2,500-square-foot manufactured home as beautiful inside as any custom build I had seen. It had everything we needed, and when we customized the exterior with limestone to match our old home, including the mailbox, I felt a surprising sense of pride.

We saved thousands of dollars, and more importantly, we finally began shedding our debt.

Yet, I still felt a pang of embarrassment when people asked about our home. I rarely told anyone that it was a manufactured house, as if I had something to hide. Society had ingrained in me that success meant having a grand house, a high-status lifestyle, and a never-ending climb upward.

But deep down, I knew the truth. Success wasn't about the house size or the car's brand. It was about financial freedom, about choices, about security.

The day we moved in, I felt something I hadn't felt in years; relief. We had shed the weight of unnecessary expenses and finally had financial breathing room.

For the first time in a long time, I felt a new kind of success; the kind that came from knowing we were building a future on solid ground.

Something in me had begun to stir, a restless energy I couldn't ignore. It was a feeling I recognized well, the one that had pushed me to take leaps. I missed the rush of a startup and the excitement of building something from the ground up. It was in my blood.

But this time, I was stuck.

For years, I had climbed the corporate ladder, taken on leadership roles, and mastered new systems. But now, I felt like I was running on autopilot. The challenges that once excited me had become routine, and the thought of staying in the same cycle, doing the same thing, made my stomach twist.

I needed something new. Something I could own. Something that could truly build wealth, not just a paycheck. But what?

I had tried before. So many times. Over the years, I have entered different ventures, each promising financial freedom. I let others persuade me, chasing shiny objects, convinced that the next big thing would finally work. I have invested money and poured in time, and each time, I have watched those ventures fizzle out, leaving me with nothing but regret and a drained bank account. I had been looking for the right thing in all the wrong places. This time I was determined to do it differently.

A mentor gave me profound advice: "Make a list of your skills. Prioritize them. Then highlight the ones you love doing."

I sat down with a notebook and started writing. The pattern became clear. I was great at connecting business operations with technology systems. Most consultants specialized in one or the other, but I had experience in both. And I *loved* bridging that gap, translating business needs into tech solutions, making things work better, smarter, and faster.

People told me before that I should go into consulting, but I brushed it off.

Doubt crept in.

Would I be able to find enough clients?

How would I market myself?

Could I sustain this long-term?

Would my husband support this leap?

And the biggest fear of all, *what if I failed?*

I turned to my husband, laying it all out, expecting skepticism or concern. Instead, he looked at me and said, "I think you should go for it."

That was all I needed. I resigned from my job, filed the paperwork, and launched my consulting business. For the first time in my career, I was my own boss.

At first, it worked. Clients came in. I was controlling my time and making more money than I ever had. I finally felt like I was on the right path.

Then, the market crashed. Almost overnight, retirement accounts were slashed in half, businesses cut spending, and companies that once relied on consultants started pulling back. Concern seeped in like an unwelcome guest. Could I sustain this? Consulting was contract-based, and every contract had an end date. One moment, I was booked solid; the next, I had no idea when my next paycheck would come. I was constantly on edge, carrying the weight of uncertainty.

After two years of riding the highs and lows, I made the tough decision to take a full-time position with the company I had been working with.

Some might have called it giving up, but I saw it differently. It wasn't failure—it was strategy. I learned invaluable lessons about risk, business ownership, and financial security. More importantly, I realized what I wanted and *didn't* want from my career.

By the fall of 2015, the question loomed over me like a dark cloud: *Could we retire?* I was fifty-five years old, and no matter how many times I ran the numbers, the answer remained the same—no. Debt still clung to us like a weight we couldn't shake off. Downsizing had helped, but it wasn't enough. Social Security and our 401(k) wouldn't sustain us as we had imagined. We needed more. More security. More cash flow. More control over our future.

Still searching for answers, we found ourselves sitting in a conference room in Dallas, surrounded by hundreds of other people looking for the same thing—a way forward. A woman stood at the front of the room, speaking with such conviction that it felt like her words were meant just for me.

She wasn't just talking about business strategies; she was talking about *life*; about purpose and how our choices either push us forward or hold us back. I was riveted. When she announced a three-day intensive training in Cleveland, Ohio, I turned to my husband. "We have to go," I whispered.

Six weeks later, we were sitting in another conference room in Baltimore, Maryland, with nearly a thousand other people. The speaker asked us to do a simple but sobering exercise: Write down our income, debt, and how much cash we had flowing in each month.

I knew the numbers before I even wrote them.

$350,000 in debt.

No cash-flowing assets.

Minimal savings.

I felt a wave of frustration and disbelief wash over me. How had we worked this hard for this long and still felt like we were standing in the same place? The next speaker took the stage, and suddenly, I was leaning in again, hanging on every word. He talked about tax laws, investment strategies, and ways to build wealth that I had never considered.

Then, he mentioned something that made my head snap up. Asset protection. For just $35 a month, we could have full access to a legal and tax team that could help us structure our finances properly.

I turned to the woman sitting next to me, a stranger from the UK who had been scribbling down notes as furiously as I had. "Did he just say *thirty-five dollars*?" I whispered.

Her mouth was slightly open in shock. "I think he did."

We both signed up on the spot.

A few weeks later, we were on the phone with the attorney, reviewing our finances and laying out our goals. We trimmed the fat, $400 of unnecessary spending, and started giving ten percent.

"We're thinking about selling some land to help pay off debt," I explained.

His response surprised me.

"Don't," he said. "You have better options."

He laid out sensible alternatives and ways to leverage what we already had instead of giving up valuable assets. For the first time in a long time, I felt hopeful. I had spent nearly forty years in business, managing operations, solving problems, handling budgets, and leading teams. Why wasn't I applying those same skills to building *our* financial future?

That was the moment we decided. August 2, 2016, we officially opened our business. Our goal? Ten rental properties in five years. We got to work, paying down debt while building a real estate portfolio of cash-flowing assets.

Our first purchase was a single-family home. We ran the numbers, and when the appraisal came back, it was much higher than our purchase price. That meant we could buy it with no money down. It was the perfect start.

Our second property, however, tested us in ways we never expected. We decided on a fix-and-hold strategy: buying a property, renovating it, and holding onto it as a long-term rental. I took a loan against my self-managed 401(k) to finance the renovations. The moment we started tearing into the house, the real work began. Unexpected damage surfaced. More repairs meant more money. More time. More stress. Then, in the middle of it all, my husband got injured.

At one point, I stood in the middle of the construction mess, looking at the exposed beams and torn-up floors, wondering if we had made a mistake. But we kept going. Eventually, the renovations were complete, and we listed the house for rent. That property—our most challenging project—became our best cash-flowing asset. We spent just over $60,000 on it, but it returns 21% to this day.

Five years into our real estate business, we had made significant progress, but not enough. The investments were steady, yet they weren't at the level that would fully support our lives. We had eliminated some debt, built a portfolio, and learned a great deal, but it still wasn't enough to retire comfortably. There had to be more. There had to be a better way.

One Saturday, I tuned into a Zoom call hosted by the attorney we had been working with—another opportunity to listen in and maybe learn helpful financial knowledge. As the speakers shared their insights on wealth-building strategies, real estate, and stock markets, I was captivated.

One speaker caught my attention. He was a former teacher who had made just $35,000 a year before he ventured into real estate investing. Now, his company is worth millions. He had built his fortune through various investment strategies—wholesaling, Airbnb, tax liens, foreclosures, and mobile home flipping, and now, he was teaching others how to do the same.

I had assumed I had real estate "figured out," but I had only been operating within a narrow scope. If I wanted to secure our financial future, I needed to expand my knowledge.

The program he was offering covered real estate and stock investing. We decided to invest.

I dove headfirst into stock investment training while we prepared to travel to Indianapolis to meet the real estate investment team in person. The training was unlike anything I had ever experienced. It wasn't just about numbers on a spreadsheet—it was about strategy, mindset, and understanding how to make money work *for* you instead of constantly chasing it.

The instructor was engaging, funny, and incredibly knowledgeable. He made complicated financial concepts easy to understand. Every session had me feverishly taking notes, my mind racing with new ideas.

In the evenings, networking events allowed us to meet other investors, people from all walks of life who were building their paths to financial independence. Each conversation inspired me further, reinforcing that we were on the right track. Then, on the second training day, the instructor played a video that shook me to my core.

On the screen, an elderly man stood at the entrance of a Walmart, greeting customers with a tired smile. The story behind him was devastating. He had worked for a company for nearly thirty years and planned to retire, but the company closed its doors just one year before retirement, and he was ineligible for his pension.

He lost everything. At eighty years old, he was forced to return to work, standing on his feet for hours daily, scanning receipts at Walmart to survive. Tears welled up in my eyes as I watched. This wasn't just one man's misfortune—this was the reality for millions of Americans living paycheck to paycheck. It could have been us. My husband and I exchanged a look. We didn't need to say anything. We both knew. It was time to take our business to the next level.

We sat down and wrote a two-year business plan. Our focus was clear: Expand our real estate portfolio and generate enough passive income to sustain our lifestyle. Every hour I wasn't at my job would be spent building our business.

We started by adopting a wholesale strategy. You know those text messages that say, *"We want to buy your home"*? That was us. We purchased a wholesaling program, assembled a small team, and traveled to North Carolina for hands-on training. By the end of the first day, I had a solid grasp of the process, the systems, and the execution. That night, in our hotel room, I launched our first text campaign.

When we landed in Indianapolis the following day, my phone buzzed, our first response.

Excitement surged through me. We called the seller and discussed the property, and within a few weeks, the deal was closed. We flipped the property and made $32,000. Could it be this simple?

We continued following the process, tweaking and refining it along the way. Each deal built our confidence and our momentum. Then, an opportunity presented itself—one that challenged my instincts and ultimately changed the trajectory of our business.

A fellow investor approached me about a property. It was three and a half acres of land with a detached garage and a supersized storage building. The land was gorgeous; lush, green, and private. But the house? It was a disaster.

The previous flipper had torn out the flooring, busted the concrete in the master bath, and dismantled the electrical panels. Walking through the house, I could feel the hesitation in the room. The investor wasn't sure if he could recover his investment.

I stayed quiet. My mind was already working, mapping out possibilities.

The layout was odd, but I saw what the house could become. With the right renovations, it could go from a three-bedroom, two-bath home to a more functional four-bedroom layout with an open-concept kitchen. And the land; *that* was the real opportunity. Instead of flipping the house alone, I saw a bigger picture. The land could be subdivided into four parcels, turning one deal into multiple income-generating opportunities.

I kept my thoughts to myself, knowing that if I was right, this could be a game-changer.

The following week, I worked with our local community bank to secure a loan. It was exhilarating. The thrill of putting a plan in motion and seeing potential where others saw problems reignited my passion. We proceeded with the project, selling three of the four properties and earning multiple six-figure profits.

That deal changed everything. I had spent my entire career solving problems for other companies, making them millions of dollars. Now, I was doing it for *us*.

Our portfolio was analyzed, and the results were clear, we were *financially secure*.

Even in the worst-case scenarios, we had built enough wealth to sustain us into our nineties. We wouldn't be a burden on our family. We wouldn't be dependent on government aid.

We had done it. We had changed the trajectory of our lives in just a few short years.

I felt an overwhelming sense of relief, of pride, of gratitude.

It was time. On April 8, 2022, I officially retired from my corporate job and began running our business full-time.

People often think it's too late to start over.

They say, *"I'm too old."*

"I don't have the money."

"I can't afford the training."

But those are just excuses.

We started with debt. We started without a financial cushion. Instead, we invested in *ourselves*—learning, training, and taking risks. Initially, we put our training expenses on a credit card. It was a risk but paid off, a *4,000% return* on just two deals.

Worth it? Hell yes.

Persistence is key. Today, our company manages a multi-million-dollar portfolio and continues to invest. The market is constantly changing, and we adapt. We also coach others, helping them take control of their financial futures. And every day, I thank God for the strength to persevere.

I love that I control my time. And *that* is true wealth.

GERI DIVITA

Geri is a seasoned professional with forty-five years of experience in business and entrepreneurship. In 2022, she embraced early retirement to focus on her entrepreneurial ventures, bringing her wealth of expertise to new opportunities. Geri has successfully run several small businesses and, in 2016, founded a management company that now oversees a multi-million-dollar portfolio. Her passion for real estate led her to build a diverse portfolio, paving her path to financial independence.

December 19, 2022, Geri and her husband co-founded Thrive For Life®, a non-profit organization dedicated to empowering individuals with tools and knowledge for personal and financial success. She is driven by a mission to inspire others to achieve financial freedom.

Married for thirty-eight years, Geri loves cooking, gardening, and tackling DIY projects with her husband. She is an avid traveler who enjoys exploring the world.

Visit Thrive For Life: www.thiveforlifetx.org
LinkedIn: geri-divita-pmp-a631051/
Facebook: https://www.facebook.com/geri.divita.7/
Instagram: @geri.divita

3

BETTER TO BE LUCKY, THAN TO BE GOOD...OR IS IT?

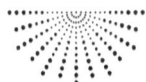

BY MELINDA GARVEY

Sometimes, it's only in hindsight that you understand how you arrived at this moment in life. Have you ever driven home, and only once you pull into the driveway do you realize you don't remember how you got there?

That's how I feel.

I've been driving for over forty years (I got my license in the womb), and while I've enjoyed the views and stopped in many places, here I am, sitting in the metaphorical driveway, wondering exactly how I got here.

So where is *here*?

Today, after twenty-two years, I'm stepping back from my day-to-day role at the company I founded, *Austin*

Woman magazine. I'm also winding down the SaaS company I founded, *On The Dot*. And because "taking a break" isn't in my DNA, I'm launching a new venture: *InHer Circle*, a peer advisory group for women.

I was lucky and born into a family that loved me fiercely and believed I hung the moon. And they told me, over and over, that hanging that moon wasn't just a dream; it was within my power. We had means, though I wouldn't fully understand that until later. I got an excellent education without a penny of debt, and my parents were my role models for deep, lasting relationships, not just with each other but with lifelong friends they cherished and nurtured.

I traveled the world and was exposed to many interests: theater, philanthropy, cooking, boating, reading, and perhaps most importantly, an interest in people; people like me, people who weren't, and people more and less fortunate.

Lately, I've been reflecting on my journey, not just on *where* I am in my life, career, and circumstances but on *who* I am and the forces that shaped me. Yes, I was lucky, but my journey wasn't all smooth sailing. Over time, I've realized that the challenges, failures, and heartbreaks may have had an even more significant impact on who I am today than the lucky breaks.

My beloved brother died of cancer at twenty-six. He's been gone thirty-two years now, but sometimes the loss still takes my breath away. At the age of twenty-four, I learned that life is painfully short. People leave you, even when it's not by choice.

And so, I've always held on tight to my people. However, I'm still learning that others don't always hold on as tightly. And when I ease my grip or let go a little to see if they'll reach back, some do, and some don't.

One of my friends often says, "Friendships have seasons." I struggle to see it that way. I think daily about the friends I've lost and wonder if I'll ever stop feeling the ache—or if that's just how it is for me. On the other hand, I have friends who've been in my life for over forty years (yes, friends from the womb), and they still feel like home.

My brother's death didn't just leave an emotional mark—it also drove me to push myself harder and influenced so many of the pivotal choices I've made. I wonder if I would've had the courage to take the risks I did: starting three companies, riding the entrepreneurial roller coaster with all its dizzying ups and downs, and living life on my terms.

There was also this sense of responsibility, this desire to be successful, even "good," as the only child left—as if I had to achieve for both of us. That pressure was entirely self-imposed, and looking back, I can smile at it, but I wouldn't change a thing. Sometimes, we have to make sense of tragedy in our own way, and if that experience drove me first to discover my passion, then pursue it, and finally succeed at it, then I'm grateful for that lesson. I know my brother would be proud.

So, how did I get to this point, sitting in my driveway wondering how I got here and where I'm going next?

I was ten years into my career, promotions, flying colors, and all, when I decided to move back to my hometown of Indianapolis to be near family after eleven years in Washington, D.C. A promising management role at a radio station (which shall remain nameless) awaited me.

I worked at an advertising agency for nearly four years right out of college, then moved on to a group of suburban daily newspapers. I eventually became the youngest VP of Sales and Marketing in a senior leadership position. But when I left D.C. for Indianapolis, it was as if the universe decided to have some fun with me.

And boy, was I about to get an education.

It all started with a series of misogynistic, arrogant, and untrustworthy men. Now, before you go thinking I'm male-bashing, understand this: I grew up surrounded by positive, encouraging male role models. My dad, brother, early bosses, and mentors supported, promoted, and pushed me to do more. So, naturally, I thought I was landing a fantastic role with a great, respected company back in Indianapolis. As far as I knew, this girl was still riding the express elevator to the top. I didn't realize that I was indeed on a ride—more like the kind where you're at the top floor of a skyscraper, and suddenly, the elevator cables snap.

My boss turned out to be a washed-up DJ with gold chains and a penchant for making lewd and suggestive comments to women in the office—particularly the sales reps who worked for me. Apparently, if you wear gold chains, leave at least three shirt buttons undone, and go by a two-letter name from your DJ days, you can call out the "hot" young sales reps. Since I was the only female manager, I quickly had a line at my door of people complaining about him. I reported him, of course, and was promptly fired. Yes, you read that right. Even the over-fifty HR director from the parent company told me I should have kept my mouth shut.

You could've knocked me over with a feather.

Remember when I said, "It's better to be lucky than good"? I'd been very lucky—I just didn't know it yet. Now, I was utterly unprepared to handle a situation like this. I wallowed in shame, in a newfound lack of confidence where once there had been plenty, and in disbelief.

So, I flew to Austin, Texas, to visit a friend and lick my wounds.

In Austin, I fell in love with the city at first sight. I immediately started looking for jobs, and within two weeks, I had a fantastic offer that included a free apartment for a year, great pay, and, best of all, I was the top dog in the office.

Or so I thought.

The senior sales rep (a woman) had applied for my job and didn't get it, so she was all too eager to derail and discredit me at every turn—something I'd never experienced in my charmed life. My boss lived in Houston but called every morning at 8:25 a.m. to ensure I was running the mandatory (and largely pointless) daily sales meeting. When I suggested we might not need this meeting daily, she clarified that I was to do as told.

And then the topper: the regional VP from Arizona decided to surprise us with a visit, and in the sales meeting, he announced, "I'm the head mother-fucker!" just in case anyone needed reminding of who was in charge. I looked around the room, half-expecting everyone to burst into laughter and acknowledge this as some caveman's attempt at breaking the ice.

But no, this was real. The looks of terror on my team's faces told me as much, and the fact that the self-proclaimed "head mother-fucker" didn't smile or slow his aggressive pacing up and down the conference room just added to the drama. So, this was the infamous "lead by intimidation" method. Huh.

After such a glorious and successful start, I began to spin out, wondering how I'd landed in this alternate universe. "Lucky" and "good" weren't cutting it this time. My confidence was gone; I questioned my every move, suffered daily migraines at work, and was generally a wreck.

So, out I went with my friend and a few of her friends to drink wine (as you do) and lament my job situation, trying to figure out what was next. But as women do so well, we started brainstorming my next move while sipping a bold cabernet.

Suddenly, my friend chimed in, "Hey! I just got back from Des Moines, Iowa!"

We all stared at her like she had three heads.

WTF? I thought. *This is my pity party, and you're talking about Des Moines, Iowa?*

But out loud, I said, "By all means, tell us about your trip."

She needed no further encouragement. "There's this magazine called *Des Moines Woman*," she said. "It tells stories of incredible, inspirational women—that's what *you* should do! You have a publishing background. And no one's doing this for women in Austin."

This was during Austin's first tech boom, and she was right—female changemakers weren't getting the spotlight. Goosebumps crept up my arms, and the hair on the back of my neck and, probably, my whole head stood up. I felt like I'd been struck by lightning. I knew, with utter certainty, this was my calling. *This* was why the universe put those back-to-back misogynistic roadblocks in my way and sent my career careening off a cliff. This was what I was meant to do.

With the support of that remarkable group of women (one of whom became my business partner), I started writing a business plan the following day. Two weeks later, I was fired/quit from my job working for "the head mother-fucker" and embarked on the journey of a lifetime. Seven months later, in September of 2002, we published the first issue of *Austin Woman*, with Amy Miller Simmons of Amy's Ice Cream on the cover.

Those early years with *Austin Woman* were surreal. We set out to give women a voice and tell their stories to inspire others, and we did it. The feedback was tremendous, and the magazine was an instant hit. We grew, added events, and did everything possible to fulfill our mission.

Then, in the blink of an eye, it was 2022, and *Austin Woman* had turned twenty. I wondered what the next twenty years would bring and thought maybe it was time to sell and "retire."

But then, it happened again. I told you I was lucky.

After a conference, I was chatting by the pool with two trusted, badass women about what might be next.

"Should I just sell?" I asked them. I was proud of how we'd championed women and leaned into diversity, equity, and inclusion (even as DEI became a "dirty" word in 2024), and I wanted that legacy to continue.

Then it struck me.

"Why must the leader be one person? What if we created a consortium of diverse women to carry on this mission?"

My friends' jaws dropped.

One said, "Are you serious? Because if you are, I'm in!"

Then the other echoed, "Me too!"

Today, *Austin Woman* is owned by eight women, including myself—two African American women, two Latina women, one Asian Pacific Islander woman, one Indian woman, and two white women. I believe we made history that day. The power of women coming together for a shared mission can make anything happen.

And a margarita or two doesn't hurt!

Somewhere in the midst of all this, I launched a tech company called *On The Dot*.

Yes, a SaaS company.

I stumbled backward in heels into tech and developed a virtual community software platform. Strangely enough, it's one of the accomplishments of which I'm most proud.

Why?

Because I never imagined a fifty-year-old English Lit major could raise capital, build software, and manage a company with, if I do say so myself, a pretty damn good product. Had I stopped to think about it, I might never have done it. But the journey taught me something invaluable: sometimes, one step after another opens the doors to achievements of which you never knew you were capable.

So what now? *Austin Woman* is on a new path, and *On The Dot* has licensed its software and wound down daily operations. While stepping away from the frenetic pace of the last twenty years felt strange, I knew I needed a break from the chaos. The stress and pressure had often left me feeling unrecognizable to myself. It took time to let go, but once I did, something interesting happened— my mind opened to new possibilities. Most importantly, I found myself getting excited about solving another problem.

If I had a dollar for every person who told me I should be a "coach" while figuring out my next move, I could have retired by now. But while I agreed I'd be good at it—I'd built two companies, restructured and sold one, raised money to fund another, and picked up countless skills as an entrepreneur over twenty-two years—something was holding me back.

I like to dive deep, both in friendships and in business. I love learning what makes people and businesses tick. When I join a nonprofit board, for example, I go all in to understand its mission to be a passionate advocate. "Coaching" or "advising" felt too surface. I know they don't have to be, but in my experience, that's often the case. Most coaches I've worked with were great at helping me manage my mental state related to business. But, none had the depth of understanding of my business to offer actionable advice, recognize opportunities, or guide me through a cash-flow crisis. You get my drift.

That's when I discovered something called Peer Advisory. It's a small group of business owners who meet monthly with a facilitator to discuss each other's businesses. The group uses its collective experience and insights to help each other overcome hurdles, grow, and scale. The problem? Most of these groups are very male-dominated—often just one or two women in a room full of men. And while I love men, let's face it: Women do things differently.

Standing up and being heard is hard when you're the minority. So, I decided to change that with the launch of *InHer Circle: Peer Advisory for Women.*

InHer Circle brings eight female business owners together as each other's personal advisory board, plus what I call "coaching with context" with me. And I'm so excited about this I can hardly stand it. I love solving problems, and now I can help other women solve theirs. And when those "other people" are women who often face more challenges raising capital, finding mentors, and securing the connections they need to grow and scale—it's a no-brainer.

Purpose is at my core. I didn't always know that. Early in my career, I liked my jobs, but I wasn't searching for some higher purpose, I didn't even know I had one until it hit me between the eyes. And once you see it, there's no going back. Purpose isn't something you can unsee.

I tried; I veered away from it when I founded a SaaS company, convinced that challenge alone would bring fulfillment. But it didn't. I'm proud of what I built in tech, but those seven years were the hardest of my life because I wasn't aligned with what truly drove me.

Now, I see that purpose isn't just about passion or success. It's about resilience, about learning to hold onto what matters through every lucky break and every heartbreaking setback. It's about embracing that mix of luck, failure, and skill, understanding that each plays its part but that growth lies in what we do with all of it. For me, purpose is about honoring my journey—and those I've lost along the way—by relentlessly pursuing what I believe in.

And in doing that, I'm finally right where I need to be.

MELINDA GARVEY

Melinda Garvey is a serial entrepreneur, founding her first company, *Austin Woman*, twenty-two years ago and then just recently executing a successful and unprecedented organizational restructure to bring on nine additional diverse female owners as partners.

"This new leadership structure allows us to realize the huge growth potential of *Austin Woman*, while at the same time ensuring the magazine continues its legacy of inclusion for generations to come." Garvey is also the founder of *On The Dot*, a B2B, SaaS Virtual Community Platform.

As Garvey winds down from her day-to-day operations role at *Austin Woman*, she is focused on her new company, *InHer Circle, Peer Advisory for Women* where she will facilitate and advise a small group of female business owners who are scaling to and beyond the million dollar mark.

Garvey is married to Kiwi husband, Kip, and together they have a seventeen-year-old son, Beck. When not with her boys or working, you will find her surrounded by inspiring women and drinking wine!

4
THE ELEPHANT'S GRAVEYARD

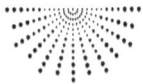

BY THERESA PORE

"How's it going in Taylor, Theresa?"

$\mathcal{T}$his was the first thing my District Manager said during our monthly check-in call. Before I could even process a response, the words poured out of my mouth:

"Sean, I feel like I live in an elephant's graveyard."

After a long pause, he asked, "What exactly do you mean by that?"

Backpedaling through my thoughts, carefully choosing my next words, I explained, "I feel so far from my purpose. My gifts and talents are wasted, and unless I do something different, I will wander off into a slow and lonely metaphorical death."

He was silent for a moment before responding carefully. "Well, we can't let that happen. Let's schedule a one-on-one meeting and talk through this."

I hadn't always felt this way. For most of my fourteen years in banking, I had been grateful for the opportunities. The bank had taken a chance on me—a nineteen-year-old, six months pregnant, recently fired from a grocery store job. They must have seen something I didn't see in myself. I was scared, inexperienced, unmarried, and had nothing to my name but a car and a good attitude.

"Yes," I agreed. "A one-on-one would be great. Let's schedule a call. But first, let me figure out where this is coming from."

That weekend, I couldn't shake the image that had surfaced so unexpectedly during my call with Sean. It lingered in my mind, haunting me with its intensity. Where did it come from? Why did it arrive at that exact moment? I didn't often pay attention to dreams or visions, but this wasn't just a passing thought. It was something more.

Saturday morning, I curled up on the white leather sofa in the sitting room of our still-barely-furnished house, a steaming cup of coffee warming my hands. Wrapped in my favorite faux-fur throw, I let the quiet settle around me.

The house was new to us—we had moved in less than a year earlier—but before we unpacked the last of our boxes, Royal, my husband, suffered a medical emergency that changed everything. Two emergency surgeries later, he was in recovery, and I spent two unexpected weeks away from work. But instead of using that time to turn our house into a home, I had been consumed with worry, navigating doctor visits and long nights of restless sleep.

As I sat in the silence of a Saturday morning, I knew I should have been decorating, arranging furniture, and making this space feel like ours. But I wasn't. Instead, I was fixated on one thing—the vision.

I opened my laptop and began typing: **Elephant's Graveyard.**

Images filled my screen—barren landscapes littered with dry bones, the remains of creatures that had once been so magnificent, now decaying under the open sky. Scenes from *The Lion King* flashed across my screen, Simba and Nala venturing into the forbidden place where the bones of the past lay forgotten. But none of it was quite what I had seen in my mind.

I refined my search: Metaphorical meaning of an elephant's graveyard.

And there it was.

The term didn't just refer to a literal place where elephants supposedly went to die—it symbolized something deeper.

It was a metaphor for spaces where obsolete, forgotten, or outdated things were left to fade away—places of neglect, abandonment, and the end of a cycle.

I stared at the words, my breath catching in my throat. That was precisely how I had been feeling. Trapped. Stagnant. Watching parts of myself waste away in a place where I no longer belonged.

God knew. He knew I needed something abrupt, something undeniable; something I couldn't ignore. And so, he gave me a clear vision.

I closed my laptop and leaned against the cushions, staring out the window at the vast sky. The message had been delivered. Now, I just had to figure out what to do with it.

Almost knocking over my coffee, I grabbed my notepad and started listing everything that had led me to this point. I was berated for missing an astronomical mortgage production goal during the recent visit from the district leadership team. My boss tore into me without reason, leaving me in tears by the time he walked out of my office.

The time nearly a year earlier, I was removed from a leadership development program for no reason other than "I wasn't on that level."

The impostor syndrome that hit every time I was asked to inspire others at district meetings, only to return to my branch and enforce micromanagement, write-ups, and performance improvement plans.

The growing realization that my idea of banking had shifted from a mission-driven service to a supercharged sales machine, where success was measured solely by quotas rather than the value we provided to people.

I had entered the Elephant's Graveyard.

Maybe leadership wasn't for me. Perhaps I needed to step back, return to a personal production role, and free myself from the weight of other people's expectations. I resigned myself to meeting with Sean to explore other roles.

"Truthfully, I wish I could have two of you; I'd put you in different markets," Sean said during our meeting. "Your attitude and desire are great. Let's start looking together if you're set on finding something different."

We ended with a plan: I would explore roles within retail sales that wouldn't require a significant pay cut; investment officer, small business development officer, or mortgage. Given my "great" mortgage skills (insert eye roll), I leaned toward business development.

I immersed myself in small business classes, treasury products, and financial reporting for six months, balancing it with my branch management duties. Finally, a VP of Small Business Development role opened up. The only downside? The territory covered

Temple, Waco, and West Williamson County, meaning I'd be far from home and my daughter's school.

I waited for Sean's call. When it came, he said, "Theresa, I've accepted your resume. I need you to meet with the City President and me this Thursday. Can you make it?"

It was the day before my stepson's Marine Corps graduation in North Carolina. My schedule was packed, but I said yes.

The week was a whirlwind of emotions, stress, and anticipation. We were preparing for a trip to watch Brenden graduate, a milestone we had all been eagerly awaiting. At the same time, we were taking the girls to Disney; a long-held dream I had placed on my vision board. I knew the end of the week would be filled with excitement and joy, and I was determined not to let the looming interview cast a shadow over it.

By Thursday morning, my schedule was packed. Meetings with my SBA loan officer on a commercial real estate deal, prepping my assistant manager for my absence, ensuring my team had their goals in place, every minute of my day was accounted for. And then, finally, it was time—the interview—the opportunity I had worked tirelessly to prepare for.

The drive from Taylor to the Executive Office in Georgetown took about forty-five minutes, longer with the late afternoon traffic. As soon as I slid into the driver's seat, I turned off the radio and let the silence settle around me. I closed my eyes for a moment and prayed.

"God, be clear. If this position is for me, make it undeniable. Let everything fall into place. But if it's not, shut the door so firmly that I don't waste time wandering in the wrong direction."

I had no idea how powerful that prayer would be—or how long He had been waiting for me to pray it. But he answered it, loud and clear.

When I arrived, the moment felt surreal. This was it. This was either my exit from the graveyard or confirmation that I was still buried in it. Walking up to the teller station, I hesitated before giving my name.

"I'm here for an interview," I said, the words feeling almost clandestine, as though I were on a secret mission. No one knew I had applied for another role.

Twenty minutes passed before Sean finally appeared. He led me to an office where the city president was seated, phone to his ear. I shook his hand, sat down, and waited. But instead of giving me his full attention, he placed his call on speaker, letting the on-hold music fill the silence.

"I'm heading out on vacation," he explained after several minutes of tinny, repetitive melodies. "Tech support needs to reprogram my phone. It won't interfere. Let's carry on."

I wasn't sure whether to nod or laugh. *This is happening,* I told myself. *Just roll with it.*

A few moments later, a knock at the door interrupted us. Sean answered it, welcoming an out-of-town guest. The three of them launched into a conversation about a regional situation while I remained seated, waiting for my interview to begin.

Minutes ticked by. Then more. Then more.

An hour after my scheduled arrival, the conversation finally turned to the role. The discussion was brief— thirty minutes, at most. They shared their thoughts, critiques of those currently in the position, and expectations. Then, without a preamble, the city president turned to me and asked, "Theresa, how long have you been with us?"

"Fifteen years," I answered.

He nodded. "Yes. That's why we brought you here today. We want to thank you for your time with us. Whether this role is for you or not, we value you."

And then—just like that—he stood, walked to the door, and held it open for me to leave.

I blinked. *Wait. What?*

In a daze, I stood, mumbled some acknowledgement, and walked toward the exit. As I stepped through the doorway, Sean lifted his hand for a high-five.

I stared at him. *What the heck just happened?*

The moment I got to my car, the dam broke. I burst into tears, the weight of it all hitting me at once. The confusion. The rejection. The surreal absurdity of the entire experience.

But I had promised myself that, no matter what happened, this interview would not interfere with our plans. And I kept that promise.

Brenden's graduation was breathtaking. I had never witnessed such an expression of pride and respect as I did during that ceremony. And Disney, after years of dreaming of taking the kids there, nothing could have prepared me for the sheer emotional exhilaration of stepping through those gates for the first time. My husband would later say he had never seen such awe and wonder on my face.

But just as quickly as it came, the trip was over. It was time to return home and face reality. And more than that, it was time to figure out how to respond to God's unmistakable answer to my prayer.

The message popped up on my screen with a familiar chime.

Don't forget about my mother-daughter Mary Kay party tomorrow, Michelle reminded me.

I groaned. I had forgotten entirely. And she knew full well that Porsha wasn't interested in skincare or makeup.

I can't come, I typed back. *I need to get my mind back in work mode and prepare for Monday.*

Seconds later, her response appeared: *Aww, Sophia was really looking forward to it. She'll have so much fun! Plus, no one else has RSVP'd yet, so I need you there.*

I sighed. She knew exactly how to rope me in. *Fine,* I wrote. *I'll go.*

Thank you!

I had been to plenty of Mary Kay parties before. I knew the routine—pampering, product demonstrations, and friendly peer pressure to make a purchase. I had recently had a Mary Kay facial and was nearly out of skincare, so I was already prepared for this night to cost me something.

But from the moment I arrived, I could sense something was different.

It wasn't just the products or the party atmosphere, it was the way they were presented, the energy in the room, the enthusiasm in the woman leading it. She was a sales director, brimming with joy, talking about her dreams of earning a pink Cadillac, breaking glass ceilings, and leaving her high-profile job at IBM to take her Mary Kay business to the next level.

Something outside banking caught my curiosity for the first time in a long time.

Could women make money doing this? Could someone love this so much that they would trade an executive career for it? Skincare? Really?

That curiosity led me to do something unexpected. Before the night was over, I had signed up as an independent beauty consultant. At first, it was just for the discount on my skincare set. But within days, I had my own business, my own inventory, and everything I needed to "try it out."

That "try" quickly turned into passion.

I threw myself into it, fully embodying the role. My lunch breaks became time for facials. My Tuesday evenings were spent driving to Austin—a commitment in itself. Every free moment, I devoured books about Mary Kay, the company, the products, and the powerhouse women behind it.

Then, in August, I attended my first seminar. Michelle and I went together, splitting a hotel room and shopping for new dresses for the celebration events. I had never experienced anything like it. The energy in the rooms was electric. Thousands of women were hugging, laughing, and celebrating with each other. Success stories filled the air—women who had changed their lives, built businesses, and discovered freedom.

And then, the moment arrived. The top three national sales directors took the stage. The crowd hushed. All eyes locked onto them as they seemed to glide across the floor. Their presence was mesmerizing, their words powerful.

Then, in an instant, something shifted. I wasn't just watching them anymore.

I saw myself on that stage. I was the one speaking. I could see every face in the audience—ten thousand women glowing with something radiant from within. I could feel their energy, their light, their hope.

And then—just as quickly—it was gone.

I sat frozen in my seat, heart pounding. God had just given me a vision. He was planting a seed, a glimpse of a new direction for my life. But now, the question was... would I honor it? Would I follow Him the way I had before, even if it meant walking into the unknown?

What if?

The question wouldn't leave me alone.

What if I used the skills I had built over fifteen years in banking to grow my business?

What if I had the freedom and flexibility Mary Kay promised?

What if I could help my husband expand our home services company?

What if I created my schedule and lived intentionally— like the women on that stage?

For months, the questions wouldn't stop.

And then, the confirmations began. Messages from friends, songs that spoke directly to me, and words of encouragement all pointed me toward something more significant.

Then came Sunday, September 4, 2016.

At church that morning, a missionary named Glenn Parker delivered a message that sent a wave through the congregation. When I stepped forward for prayer, he paused in front of me.

"I know what anointing feels like," he said. "And the anointing is all over you."

Tears welled in my eyes.

"God is waiting on you to move," he continued. "He has called you to another place to use you, but you must be willing to move."

The words shattered every doubt, every hesitation. I dropped to my knees, surrendering to what I already knew in my heart.

Two days later, after a long day of sitting on an interview board, encouraging others to join the company I was about to leave, I called Sean.

"I'm ready to resign."

The reality hit in waves. At the time, I managed two branches—two days a week in Round Rock and three in Taylor. Leaving wasn't easy, but I made a plan. I would stay through the quarter to earn my final commission and help my husband prepare for the busy season at our chimney company. We needed a financial cushion as my salary disappeared.

And then, the day came. Sean supported me and stood by me as I closed this chapter. We grabbed some of Taylor's famous BBQ and soaked in the moment.

After sixteen years, my life as a banker ended and my journey as an entrepreneur began.

Freedom felt good. I fully embraced the make-your-own schedule, at least for a few weeks. Then fear kicked in. Our chimney business was making enough to pay a few employees a decent hourly wage, but Royal was not used to taking a salary. The strain on our family business became real when we increased his pay to match my executive salary. I knew that if I didn't get to work supporting him and building the business, it wouldn't be long before we would both be looking for a job. My fight-

or-flight brain kicked in, and my management muscle went to work.

At first, Royal's lovely wife, whom employees had seen on occasional visits and office parties, was welcomed with open arms. But after a few weeks of reality kicking in—that we were in business to make money and needed to build processes around profitability—the "D" personality took over again, and I wasn't considered the nice one anymore. I became the bossy one.

The micromanagement tendencies I had been forced into at the bank took over, and I traded one dreaded role for another. The difference was that I didn't have to go home with my old boss—I only had to see him on quarterly visits and monthly meetings. Now, the struggle I was beginning to have was with my husband, who had very different leadership tendencies and communication skills than I did. This conflict became evident. While we tried to mask it, it wasn't long before our employees saw the fruits of our frustrations, and a few even began to play us against one another.

My plan to control the flow by waiting until the business could afford my salary backfired. Entering a new role in our own business, where all the income and responsibilities lay on us, was not a good idea during our busy season when we were trying to survive the flow.

In those first few months, I kept thinking, *Where is my book of operations (BOB, as we called it at the bank) to tell me what to do?* I ran into so many problems that I couldn't answer. I quickly learned that I was in an industry I knew nothing about, even though it had been in my family for three decades. I was drowning and needed to pull myself together.

As spring rolled around the corner and tax season arrived, my accountant asked for our business financials, and once again, I was like, wait, who is doing that for us? Who do I call? Employee issues started to arise, and it was time to say goodbye to a few who didn't align with where we were going as a company. We got calls from Texas Workforce about unemployment claims, and once again, I was lost as to who to turn to.

Two of my favorite experiences (insert sarcasm here): Getting a phone call from my accounts receivables rep while I was at Walmart picking up office supplies, saying, "Theresa, where are you? I need you to come back to the office. An armed IRS agent is here, and he won't leave until he talks to you or Royal."

Or the knock on the door from the nicely dressed courier who handed me a large letter-sized envelope saying, "You have been served," launching us into a three-year lawsuit only to get the response from my Insurance Agent that we didn't have proper coverage for this type of work, and you are responsible for the entire bill and the legal fees...

This was not turning out the way I had anticipated. Kidding, but not kidding; I would look at Royal almost daily and ask, "Who is running this show?" I wondered in amazement what in the world had kept us going up to this point. Thing after thing was falling through the cracks, but now it was my fault and my responsibility to fix it. There was no one to turn to, blame, or counsel with—it was our cake, and we had to eat it.

I remember the day so clearly.

Royal and I sat across from each other in yet another "oh crap" strategy session; one of those meetings where the weight of our business struggles felt heavier than we could carry.

The problems were evident, but the solutions? Those felt just beyond our grasp.

At some point in the conversation, I stopped. "Go get me a whiteboard," I told him. "A huge one."

Minutes later, he returned, and I picked up a marker, determined to map out a way forward. I drew a diagram, placing Royal at the center and sketching a vision for what our business should look like, not just what we managed in survival mode but what we needed to thrive.

One by one, I began outlining the positions we lacked—roles crucial to any business's success but entirely out of reach for our budget. Marketing. Coaching. Finance. Funding. Taxes. Human Resources. Sales Partners.

Legal. Asset Protection. Insurance. Training & Development.

I stepped back and stared at the board. These were all gaps. Gaps that were keeping us from scaling, keeping us stuck in the cycle of reaction instead of strategy.

Then, the lightbulb moment. We might not be able to hire these positions outright, but what if we built something different?

Over the next few months, I turned to my network—the relationships I had cultivated throughout my banking career. Instead of trying to fill these roles internally, I partnered with people whose businesses already specialized in the areas where we needed support.

I started with a business coach, a marketing firm, and a human resources expert.

And then, a pattern emerged: Every time we made one strategic addition, our business gained traction. With every step forward, we added another trusted advisor to our "board business model." This approach transformed everything.

Suddenly, we had clarity. We identified weak spots before they became breakdowns. We cleaned up broken systems. We created new ones where none had existed. And when the pandemic hit—a time that crushed so many small businesses—we didn't just survive. We stayed focused. We grew.

What started as a desperate attempt to plug holes became a blueprint for success. We started seeing major improvement in business, and finally, I would be able to shift my focus back to Mary Kay, or so I thought.... For some unknown reason, even though I had made improvements at Top Hat and my focus could shift, I found that I was now running into new walls.

The pattern was no longer behind the scenes, it was no longer hidden in an external force. It was in me.

I remember the day so clearly. I was awake early on a Sunday morning, drinking a cup of coffee and scrolling on social media. As I walked through the newly remodeled kitchen and coffee bar to pour a fresh cup, something caught my eye. An infomercial titled "The Blissful Breadwinner" immediately, I thought, how in the heck do those two phrases go together? Blissful and breadwinner, so I pushed play.

A beautiful Australian voice began to narrate stories of women who had reached a place called burnout. A place where they felt that the only option was to shut down, to step out of the chaos of the world and reclaim their peace.

Without missing a beat, she ended the video with an option to jump on a call and learn about how to become a "blissful breadwinner," how to maintain the life of achievement without sacrificing all that matters in the process. I took her up on the free chat and within minutes, for the first time in my forty years in life, I felt seen, I felt heard, and I felt like she could help me rediscover my value.

For the next few years, I went into a spiritual "be still" era. I did the work that the coach recommended, not for a job, not for a boss, not for anyone or any other reason, but to discover who I truly was. This led to a process of examining areas of my life that I had buried for fear of being found out, areas of my life where hurts and pain had caused me to build walls around my heart, keeping people out. It led me on a journey of opening up old trauma wounds and revisiting defining moments and analyzing them from a whole and healed place rather than from the lens that I had experienced them in.

It led me to a journey of becoming healthy in mind, body, and spirit, and finally into a community where I felt free to simply be me. Not to perform, not to "fake it til you make it," but to bring my authentic self.

This healing journey was so necessary, yet I didn't even know it was what I needed to heal from my past. It also became *the* thing that held me together during the next few years as we faced horrific, unthinkable challenges in our family that would knock the wind out of us, all leading up to a final blow, losing my mom to cancer in October of 2023.

As I began putting pieces together coming home from her funeral, I clung on to a shirt that she wore so many times over her battle with pride. This shirt was royal blue and had a picture of Rosie the Riveter saying "lung cancer warrior" in the top corner and "unbreakable" on the bottom.

Looking in my bathroom mirror as I wore the shirt, I started to cry out to God and said, "Why God, why did *she* have to break?" Immediately, the answer was dropped in my spirit that said, "Many times in life you will run into things that will bend you, challenge you, crush you and make you feel like you are breaking—but with the right foundation, until it is time to come home, you will remain unbreakable."

That was it. I got the message. God just revealed to me my purpose.

All of the moments in life so far had come to this one final place, and I knew what he was telling me. As I began to meditate on the word foundation that he used, I began to discover what sustained me during the burnout season and what foundation pillars he established to give me a solid foundation.

Self-Discovery.

Mindset/ Mindshifting.

Beliefs.

Trauma/ Defining Moments.

Health.

Community.

Purpose.

I learned that the challenges I faced, once worked through in a systematic way, allowed me to take back my power and discover who the real Theresa Pore was. My life's purpose became helping others do the same.

And with it, a new opportunity was born: UnBreakable Enterprises, LLC.

Under UnBreakable Enterprises, we launched an UnBreakable Women's Conference with a UnBreakable Life coaching program that walked individuals through the seven pillars and established the foundation of an UnBreakable Life.

We launched UnBreakable Health, a platform to help individuals become healthy; mind, body, and spirit. We taught them to embrace their unique bodies and be empowered to make health decisions based on their DNA, sensitivities, and hormonal makeup.

This program was eye-opening for so many who were conditioned to believe they had limited power regarding their health. We revealed the lies, agendas, and propaganda used by food and drug companies to provide the truth about what health and healing can be for each person uniquely. We weren't designed to be a sick nation; overweight and full of brain fog and mental illnesses. Our program helps individuals get to the root of all these issues and re-establish their health.

We launched UnBreakable Men, a platform for men to have a community and reclaim their identity and masculine power. A community for men to have a support system that encourages communication, healing, and strength as a gift, not a weakness.

All over the world, men, women, and children are struggling and are on the verge of burnout or breakdown. Our UnBreakable Life programs were designed to give them a holistic approach to healing with practical tools, communities, and resources to maintain and thrive in challenging times.

As our conferences and programs began to evolve, we found a common theme—an issue that we wanted to address head-on. As our clients began to heal, grow, and, as I call it, "take back their power," they needed additional tools and resources to enable their growth to continue after our program.

As they got stronger, healthier, and mentally tougher, we found that their external support needed assistance as well. Studies show that when healing begins, our patterns, behaviours, and higher-level thinking increase, which may reveal insecurities in relationships, both internal and external.

We couldn't stop at the UnBreakable Life Program; we wanted to go all in. We needed to extend our support to the legs of life, such as marriages, relationships, children, families, and businesses.

This extension allows us to meet people where they are and help them feel seen, valued, and heard.

Our UnBreakable Marriage/Relationships focus on the Five Pillars of: Intimacy, Communication, Service, Connection, and Unity.

One of the biggest challenges we face today is division when faced with adversity. We go into hustle mode and often forget about the importance of making those who are committed to us feel important.

Intimacy and communication are typically the first to go, which leads to a loss of connection and unity. We teach couples how to honor each other in the growth process and maintain these important aspects of the relationship, no matter what comes their way.

UnBreakable Families focuses on the Five Pillars of: Communication Autonomy, Connection, Tradition, and Legacy.

As the family goes, so goes the community, the nation, and the world. By exploring these pillars, we equip families with tools and resources for celebrating who they are uniquely and collectively and empower them to create their own traditions and legacy.

Finally, Unbreakable Business: Too many small business owners feel like they're drowning, overwhelmed by the moving parts of business that seem unimportant...until they suddenly become life-or-death decisions.

I knew what that felt like. I also knew that most entrepreneurs weren't failing because of a lack of passion. They were failing due to a lack of structure, and no one had ever taught them the foundational business skills that separate thriving companies from struggling ones.

UnBreakable Business focuses on the Three Pillars of Education: Collaboration, Motivation, and the 12 Spokes of Business™—as I laid out on my whiteboard experiment—to help small businesses stay connected with and on top of all business areas.

This work became my greatest joy. I was once asked what I want to be remembered for. The answer was simple. I want people to say, "because of Theresa Pore and her work, I felt seen, and because I was seen, I was empowered to take back my power." We get to witness that every day.

I feel deeply called to help others embrace their God-given dreams with a solid foundation. Because here's the truth—life isn't easy, purpose rarely comes without pain, business doesn't come with a book of operations, and families are under attack—but are worth fighting for.

We weren't designed to wander off into the desert simply waiting to pass on, but rather to complete our own unique purpose and help others do the same.

Looking back, I am thankful for the Elephant Graveyard experience and vision—when I knew I had to step into my purpose, no matter how terrifying. Without it, I wouldn't have had the courage to burn the boats and charge forward into the life I was meant to live.

THERESA PORE

As a keynote speaker, trainer, bestselling author, and coach, Theresa uses life lessons from two decades of marriage, sixteen years of work in the financial services industry, community leadership roles, developing and running business-to-business networking organizations, and successfully navigating mergers and acquisitions, owner operating several businesses to help men and women build resilience and create their success.

Theresa hosts the Unbreakable Women's Conference™, which focuses on helping women "take back their power" by turning broken pieces into purpose.

Theresa and her husband, Royal, founded UnBreakable Enterprises LLC, which takes the elements of UnBreakable Life™ (self-discovery, mindset, personal beliefs, defining moments/ trauma, health, community, and purpose) and makes them universal to relationships, businesses, marriages, and families.

Theresa's Mission: "Helping you live your life's purpose by living your life on purpose."

Visit UnBreakable Business:
www.unbreakable-business.com
Learn about the UnBreakable Women's Conference:
www.unbreakablewomensconference.com
Learn about Theresa Pore: www.theresapore.com
LinkedIn: theresa-pore-256b29126

5

WOMAN RISING

BY JENNIFER JOHNSON

*W*ith my sneakers laced tightly and my high heels tucked in my shoulder bag, this girl from small-town Texas had journeyed far from cleaning bays at my parents' car wash. My mission was clear: Today was my day to win. The crisp city air carried a promise, and the sun greeted me warmly each time I crossed avenues free of towering buildings. Mary J. Blige's "I Feel Good" pumped through my headphones, providing the soundtrack to my determination.

Turning right onto Sixth Avenue from 43rd Street, I was moments away from stepping into the marble and granite palace of one of New York City's iconic "white shoe" law firms. I'd prepared meticulously, studying the attendee list, memorizing bios, rehearsing my pitch, and searching for common ground. I knew the stakes. This was the meeting that mattered.

After the usual security checkpoint ritual—a visitor's badge clipped to my jacket—I ascended to the fifty-sixth floor. In a discreet corner, I swapped comfort for confidence, stepping into my heels. I boarded the elevator, which surged upward, a subtle pop in my ears marking my ascent.

The doors opened to a two-story, windowless lobby, where expensive floral arrangements towered over mahogany tables. A receptionist smiled mechanically as I introduced myself. Guided to a seating area resembling a well-appointed living room, I exhaled slowly, centering myself. The meeting was set for 9:30 a.m., and I'd arrived precisely ten minutes early—punctual, professional, and prepared.

But time ticked on; 9:35 a.m., then 9:42 a.m. Still no one. At 9:50 a.m., voices spilled into the lobby; the meeting before mine had run late. I recognized my competition instantly as he received enthusiastic handshakes and friendly pats on the back, promises of lunches to come echoing down the hall.

Finally, the conference room door opened, but no one stepped forward to welcome me. A voice called out flatly across the expansive space, "Jennifer, please come in."

I entered with my shoulders back, my smile confident. Inside, eight men waited at an expansive marble table wearing nearly identical custom-tailored suits. No one stood or moved, and no introductions were offered. I walked the runway across the room to the chair clearly designated for me, distributing my business card and greeting each one by name. A muttered "Wow" and an amused "No kidding" drifted across the table, more commentary than connection.

Then, as I began to take my seat, I sank awkwardly low. The chair was as close to the ground as the setting would allow. Heat rose in my cheeks as I stood to adjust it, aware of their silent amusement. Was this intentional? Were they trying to throw me off? Undoubtedly.

Taking a deep breath, I steadied myself and attempted rapport, my professionalism steadfast despite feeling their scrutiny like a spotlight. I distributed laminated placemats—a sales technique borrowed from a friend—to highlight my firm's exceptional capabilities. They nodded and smirked, exchanging subtle glances as I reclaimed my chair.

"So," one finally said, his tone dripping with condescension, "where are you from?"

"I've lived here seven years," I responded calmly, "but originally, Texas."

"You don't have an accent."

I flashed a smile. "I trained as a singer. Diction lessons neutralized it. But I can bring it back if y'all prefer." My quick reply drew polite chuckles, but nothing genuine.

"Why should we hire you?"

I launched confidently into my credentials, showcasing my thorough understanding of their firm, its market challenges, and my proven ability to deliver results. "What exactly are you looking for in a consultant?" I asked.

Their answer mirrored everything I had just articulated.

One man tapped my carefully crafted placemat, eyebrows raised. "Impressive. Mind if I share it with our marketing folks?"

"Of course," I replied, clinging to optimism.

Yet, less than twenty-five minutes later, restless shifts and watch-checking signaled it was over. "Any more questions for her?" someone asked. Not for Jennifer—for her. Silence sealed my fate.

I thanked them, reiterated my interest, and asked about their decision timeline. Vague assurances followed, but no one offered to escort me out. Unlike my predecessor, I left alone, unacknowledged.

Two weeks later, through whispers in my network, I discovered the inevitable: they had hired the man before me. They knew him. It was never really a contest. Qualified or not, prepared or not, I'd been summoned presumably to tick a box.

So many questions lingered. Why invite me only to belittle my preparation and mock my ambition? Why diminish me in subtle, calculated ways—lowering chairs, refusing eye contact, minimizing my presence to a dismissive pronoun? I wasn't the girl who cleaned car washes under a sweltering Texas sun. Not anymore.

Getting from There to Here

I had originally planned to go to law school, but decided to work inside a law firm to see what it was like, so I took a job running the firm's summer internship program and handling law student recruitment.

After spending time in the firm, I started noticing the lawyers—heads down all day, buried in paperwork and case law. Every so often, one would pop up like a meerkat, scanning the horizon from behind towering stacks of legal books, eyes sharp with the same mix of curiosity and caution, before disappearing back into their burrows of briefs and memos. Watching that day after day made me rethink whether that was the life I wanted.

I realized I loved recruiting, especially getting to know people, understanding their interests, and then making the right connections. It felt a lot like solving a puzzle, something I've always enjoyed. Finding the perfect fit between a person's background and someone who could benefit from their expertise became both a challenge and a reward.

After a few years at the law firm, I made what some called a bold decision to pack up and move from Texas to New York City in 2004. And I'm not exaggerating when I say the only person I knew in the entire city was the one who had interviewed me for the job I had just accepted. Looking back, I realize that was the first step in a journey built on trust in myself. It took me a long while to understand this.

I spent the next six years working for this well-established search firm, honing my "intrapreneur" mindset in recruiting business professionals for law firms, not lawyers. While I was not an owner, I worked inside the business as if I were. Thinking ahead, anticipating how things could go sideways, going the extra mile to put a personal touch on every email, working outside of normal business hours to accommodate my client's needs, and volunteering after hours for industry boards and committees. Thinking about my clients and candidates, even when I didn't need or want anything from them. Building trusted relationships. One at a time. I became a connector of people, ideas, venues, and aspirations.

After feedback from several clients that I was getting results for them no other had been able to do, I was encouraged by the same group that I should consider starting my own business and tailoring search services for clients under my own brand. While many of my day-to-day points of contact for client work were women, selling at the c-suite was much harder because the buyers of executive search services at the highest level are typically men, and the search industry, my competition, are predominantly men. I had an uphill road to climb.

Having seen my parents start and end several businesses over the years, and been a part of their journey and points of learning, I felt I had the pre-qualified foundational experience that provided me with the confidence that I could go out on my own. I decided to do it.

April 9, 2011 was the day. I pulled together a website, sent out an email to all of my contacts and then sat at my desk praying that the phone would ring. The first few days were filled with many calls from people congratulating me on taking the step.

On day four "the" call came. Someone I had worked with for years before had a position for me to fill on their team. I was officially in business. For the first couple of years it was me, myself and I serving in all the roles you could imagine in a business. I originated the client, delivered the service, shepherded relationships, sent the invoices, collected the payments, figured out how to pay corporate taxes and renew website URLs.

I slowly began adding others to the team to source candidates and fulfill the inbound workload, and administer the increasingly complex business infrastructure. After four years of hard work, tireless hours, and dedication, I cracked a seven-figure gross revenue.

I would be remiss if I didn't acknowledge the influential people of all genders, but especially a couple of men, who helped me exponentially along the way.

From a partner in the law firm I learned the hard way about the distinct pecking order of a corporation (to be clear, I was on the very bottom of the totem pole) but the same man also shepherded me to make a presentation to the firm's leadership with an idea I had to up our recruitment game resulting in a big promotion.

Or the former boss who was now at a different firm that hired my firm to work on an important search despite competitors with more experience- the same man who offered to call the CEO of another firm to vouch for my professionalism and capabilities to help seal the deal on a new project I had set my sites on resulting in a win.

There are good people out there who do, in fact, want to see you succeed. Genuinely and selflessly. The key is to hang onto these and not let the bad outshine the good.

Power Plays and Personal Growth

Returning to the conference room scene, intentional or not, those lowered chairs shrunk me instantly. Confident, capable Jennifer—the woman who'd worked tirelessly to earn her reputation—vanished, replaced by the lonely sixth-grader who ate lunch in a bathroom stall because her "friends" said there was no room despite the empty chair.

The internal monologue began: *You're in over your head. You don't belong here.* Over time, these microaggressions reinforced the notion that others somehow held power over my place at the table.

The archetype of men beating their proverbial chests was everywhere. Getting new tires (forget about buying a car, that's the worst). Sideline conversations at my kid's soccer game. A plumber coming to fix the bathtub. A board meeting for a nonprofit I served on. Everywhere.

It's interesting how I was regularly invited into these spaces—this must mean I was on to something, right? And yet, I was subtly made to feel undeserving of being there.

Take the "exclusive" networking group I joined. I was the first woman ever invited. On my first day, they asked me to introduce myself and share my company's plans. After my elevator pitch, one of the men started grilling me with hyper-specific financial questions—sales pipelines, EBITDA (what?). Then he smiled and said, "Well, you sure have built yourself a nice little business. You should be proud."

I'm almost sure he meant it as a compliment. But would he have said that to one of the men in the group?

Later, he called me directly. He claimed to have business referrals, but instead, he told me my business was "impressive" and then—wait for it—offered me a job at his firm so I could turn my "cute lifestyle business" into something "real."

"Well, this took an unexpected turn," I replied dryly.

He said, "I have some advice for you, you should always be prepared for a conversation to go in any direction."

I responded, "Do you realize how insulting you sound?"

"Oh, I don't mean it that way," he replied. "It's just that your business is really interesting, and I think it could be better."

Better.

All this from a man I had spent no more than an hour with in a group setting—plus this twenty-minute phone call.

Who is he to decide what is or isn't interesting? What is or isn't better? With just a few words, he pulled me back to that old, familiar place where I wasn't good enough. But lucky me, he could make it all better.

In thinking back to the boardroom of bullies, I found that I began understanding a profound truth: their reactions were less about my inadequacies than their own collective insecurities. Their power relied on my willingness to shrink. And I was done shrinking.

Yes, the good ol' boys' network was alive and thriving, but so was I. Everyone who underestimated me became fuel to propel me further. I knew I had value. And so, I had trained myself to withstand rejection.

Know Thyself

Several years ago, I realized that my weekly commitment to therapy was a powerful commitment to myself. Even if I didn't always make time for self-care in other ways, therapy helped me reflect on the experiences I encountered, including being given "constructive criticism" (by a man) that I was "really just too much and should consider toning it down in certain situations."

Through it all, I've seen each experience placed before me as practice for what's next. To make me more resilient.

The reality is that we are born into a movie well into its plot, playing supporting roles whether we like it or not. It's not until we understand where we came from—our original family unit—that we recognize how it has shaped how we respond to situations and people.

For me, the programming to keep moving came from being the child of parents who built businesses that required constant upkeep to stay competitive. Daily cleaning of each car wash bay, emptying the trash cans filled with the litter people dumped from their trunks. Monthly maintenance of the vacuums that sucked up dirt, debris, numerous pennies and dimes—and occasionally, a single diamond earring!

Standing in the sun for hours, changing dollars into quarters to keep the line moving. There was always something to do seven days a week, 365 days a year. Not just to keep things running, but to make sure they ran well so customers would return.

We all have a part of ourselves that wants to protect and defend us from perceived threats. And another part that wants to escape from anything hard or uncomfortable—pick a vice, any vice. To understand what activates each of these parts is key to gaining resilience. What makes you want to fight? What makes you want to take flight? What makes you freeze?

I spend a lot of time observing people, their word choices, actions, and how they move through the world, to build a picture of the whole puzzle. Over time, I started noticing shifts. I moved from feeling defensive and dismissing myself to trusting myself and dismissing others' attempts to diminish me. I realized that my lived experiences and responses to them led me to my true and wise self—my north star.

And while I still slip into protection mode on occasion, I trust myself enough to take more risks, even if that means getting a response I don't like. Because through allowing myself to be in uncomfortable scenarios I gain the practice to know I'd be okay.

"No One Can Make You Feel Inferior Except Yourself" - Eleanor Roosevelt

A decade into owning my business, I finally landed a meeting with a C-suite executive who had eluded me for years. Given the timing of his outreach, I assumed he was interested in a high-profile project my firm was working on. But in our meeting, he denied this. He said he was just, "curious about the market." Then he asked me to tell him more.

I explained what my client needed in their next leader—and found myself shrinking.

Why was I doing this? What had he said or done to make me question my expertise?

Then, to my horror, I heard the words come out of my mouth: "I'm saying all this to prove I know what I'm talking about."

I couldn't believe it. After *twenty years,* I had just spoken words that went *completely* against what I knew to be true about myself. I didn't need to prove myself to *him.* If anything, it was the other way around!

And yet, somewhere along the way, I had built a narrative that he was mighty, and I was just—little 'ol me.

Had I diminished myself?

I think I had.

Many years earlier, in that conference room in New York, a group of players in a similar scenario left me feeling small. But this time? *This* was all me.

Rather than spiral into shame and blame, I paused and acknowledged the moment. I reminded myself that rewiring deeply rooted patterns takes time. Intentional practice, patience, and awareness became my tools for personal growth.

I now trust myself instead of shrinking in response to intimidation tactics. I also learned this: If people are willing to pay me for my expertise—and do so repeatedly—I must have value. I must have something to say. Not only did I believe this, but I was also rewarded financially for it.

Another lesson I've picked up? Most people are entirely unaware of how their words come across. And many of them have selective memory. I now find it hilarious when I meet someone for the third time, and they do not recall meeting me. Out of sight, out of mind. I don't take it personally anymore.

Fast forward fifteen years. I got an urgent call from the same firm in New York that had picked the other guy all those years ago. They wanted me to present my capabilities for consideration in hiring a new C-suite executive.

I asked, "When and where?"

I entered confidently; this meeting was unmistakably different. This time, I was escorted to the elevator with a handshake and said the words I'd long known I deserved: "The business is yours."

Walking out, head held high, I felt the weight of the past slip away. There was no more shrinking, no more invisible armies dictating the narrative, only a clear, unshakable knowing that I belonged precisely where I stood, flourishing despite every attempt to diminish me.

I didn't see the deeper message when I watched the *Barbie* movie with my daughters for the first time. Watching it a second time, the more profound message finally resonated. Gloria's monologue struck deeply:

"I'm just so tired of watching myself and every single other woman tie herself into knots so people will like us."

I spend a lot of time counseling people in my network as they navigate career moves, some through our firm, but many on their own in a different industry or through a different firm. They tell me stories about how life events have changed their trajectory, or a company didn't meet with them because of a certain detail on their resume.

Anyone who knows me will have heard me say, "Well, if they don't like it, you don't want to work there anyway" and "It's their loss!". The right opportunity to work with the right people will present itself so long as you are aware and accepting of the parts of yourself that drive you to run or to hide.

In the past twenty-five years of working, I have finally learned not to linger on rejections but to cherish the affirmations. For all the no's I get along the way, I hold onto the yes's. If someone doesn't see—or refuses to see—the value I bring, I know others will, and they are where I focus my superpowers.

JENNIFER JOHNSON

Jennifer has built a career on resilience—thriving despite systemic bias, personal setbacks, and the microaggressions that often diminish professional women. Rather than letting these challenges define her, she has transformed them into fuel for growth, success, and empowerment.

As CEO of Calibrate, Jennifer has shattered barriers, cultivated a powerful network of multi-industry leaders, and established a brand that elevates overlooked business services professionals. Her firm is a go-to partner for industry-leading strategies and executive search, helping clients navigate complex organizational structures and achieve their most critical business objectives.

Learn about Calibrate: calibrate-strategies.com

6

FINDING PURPOSE IN THE GAPS

BY SHELLEY LARSEN

*O*n my tiptoes at seven years old, I could barely see over the handles of the wheelchair I was pushing. Excited and determined, I headed toward the smell of cafeteria rolls, overcooked meat and warm vegetables. My primary task was simple: Helping residents in wheelchairs navigate the halls, carefully steering around others meandering with canes and walkers toward the dining hall. The smiles, hugs, and looks of adoration from the residents, including my great-grandmother, motivated me to help as many as possible.

Other important tasks during my visits included brushing my grandmother's long silver hair and dancing with Mr. Bojangles, a resident known for spreading cheer through song and dance.

Throughout my childhood, I continued to be drawn to helping others. It was as natural as breathing. Whether it was tending to a scraped knee, standing up for friends who were being bullied, or playing the role of helper in the kitchen at Grandma's, I always felt an innate pull toward easing the burdens of those around me. This inclination wasn't something I consciously chose. It was a thread that wove itself seamlessly through my childhood years, binding together small everyday moments into a larger pattern of compassion and service.

As I grew into my teen years, I eagerly volunteered at vacation Bible school, at a summer camp for children with disabilities, and I delivered food trays in the local hospital as a candy striper. I loved traveling with my church on mission trips to build homes and churches.

At nineteen, I was racking my brain, trying to figure out my next steps in life and the path I should take with school and career. I was in classes at the local junior college, but I needed a plan and to choose a major. How would I figure this out? Quiet reflection on my life experiences gave me the information I needed to make the decision. I felt a sense of purpose when I was helping others.

Even in the simplest acts, like assisting an elderly person to their car or distracting a fussy baby while in the check-out line at the grocery store, I genuinely enjoyed helping others. Looking back, I can see how the experiences of helping others shaped my perspective on life. They instilled in me a deep appreciation for human connection and the power of kindness, which influenced my path in profound ways. Helping others wasn't just something I did, it became a part of who I was. This guiding principle carried me forward into my career choice and into adulthood.

I would become a nurse!

Nursing school was a whirlwind of knowledge, discovery, and transformation, opening a wide array of ideas on how to help others. My favorite topic during pre-nursing was nutrition, exploring the importance of a balanced life with healthy foods and exercise. Before that, most of my wellness knowledge had come from popular health magazines. I still had a lot to learn. Nursing school provided a deeper understanding of critical thinking and assessment skills, covered various nursing specialties, and introduced a broad range of nursing theories. We built camaraderie among classmates and shared eye-opening experiences during clinical rotations.

After college, in my first job as a critical care nurse, shift changes involved thirty minutes of detailed information exchange required to take over care of two intensive care patients. The monitors' rhythmic heartbeats, alarm notifications, and the steady whir of blood pressure cuffs every five minutes formed a constant background noise amid nurses' conversations. Those were the longest and busiest twelve hours of my life. After hours spent caring for and bathing two critically ill patients, I had to sit down and chart, struggling to stay awake at 4:30 a.m.

Despite the intensity, I loved the excitement and continued working in critical care for five years. It felt surreal at times, particularly when a patient passed away or miraculously woke up.

As thrilling as the ICU was, it had also revealed a problematic truth: Many of my patients never heard my voice, never felt my touch in a moment of reassurance. They were asleep, sedated, unaware of the care being poured into them. I longed to connect, to be a source of comfort, not just a provider of treatment.

Eventually, I moved away from the ICU and transitioned into outpatient surgery, where I assisted and comforted patients before, during, and after surgery.

I worked happily in outpatient surgery for many years. Over time, the stress of my profession and the latest job I was working on weighed heavily on my mind, body, and spirit. My chest felt heavy, my heart raced, and I struggled to catch my breath.

My mind spun endlessly with chatter, dread, and gloom as Sunday night approached, knowing I faced another week filled with stress, overwhelm, and despair. My husband watched helplessly as I cycled through emotional outbursts, irritability, and tearful breakdowns, waves of despair washing over me. Panic would set in, then momentarily fade, only for another intense emotion to rise again. I'd pace and procrastinate, trapped by overwhelm, desperately wanting to escape; but how?

This was my first experience with ongoing anxiety, triggered by burnout from my nine-to-five job. My role wasn't terrible; in fact, I genuinely enjoyed aspects of it. Becoming a director in nursing was among the highest achievements in my profession.

I'd served as clinical director for nearly six years, finding fulfillment in positively impacting others and making a difference. Arriving at the surgery center around 6:00 a.m., I'd often witness a beautiful sunrise from my office window—the vibrant red glow slowly rising above the horizon.

The early morning commute was calm, allowing me to listen to podcasts about Eckhart Tolle's book, *A New Earth: Awakening to Your Life's Purpose.* The teachings encouraged awareness of the ego's influence, embracing the present moment, and discovering one's true essence and purpose.

I believed I was fulfilling my life's purpose, yet a low-level unease gnawed deep within me, leaving me unsettled. This internal struggle persisted longer than it should have. Listening to Mr. Tolle reminded me that true presence dissolves suffering and fosters inner peace

—something I'd lost along the way. I was merely going through the motions, living for weekends, wine, travel, home renovations, or anything else to distract me from work temporarily. How had I arrived here?

I felt trapped. Despite ongoing anxiety and restlessness as a director, I planted my feet firmly in my job. Burnout had taken hold, yet I wasn't ready to look for something else. There was a familiar nudge pulling me toward discovering my purpose, echoing the feelings of my nineteen-year-old self—only this time, I was approaching fifty.

From the outside, my life appeared successful and accomplished, yet anxiety lingered. Deep down, I knew I had more significant dreams. I felt conflicted. It was time to pause, reflect on my journey, and adjust my trajectory. Something had to change. Unbeknownst to me, things were about to shift.

In March 2020, the world stopped. Covid arrived like a wave, turning everything upside down. The surgery center slowed significantly for several months because we were mandated to shut down, except for urgent cases. The following six to seven months were filled with policy and process changes and countless online meetings.

Less work gave us more time to focus on ourselves and our families. My husband and I didn't waste this precious newfound time. Even though the world had shut down, we felt more connected to friends and neighbors than we had in years. Several neighbors invited us to join them in cycling, and by April, we had bought bikes and began riding multiple times a week.

Cycling became our way of connecting socially while forming healthy habits. Throughout most of 2020, we enjoyed shorter work hours and the relaxed pace Covid brought to our lives.

However, when the surgery center reopened fully and I stepped back into my role, I realized I no longer belonged there. A lot had changed, including me. I had experienced a new sense of freedom and no longer felt aligned with the director position. Yet, despite my desire to move on, my ego kept me stuck. I believed the center couldn't operate without me, and the uncertainty of leaving my role felt daunting. But as I've learned, when God nudges, and you resist, those nudges become stronger.

I was exhausted. My most significant shortfall as director was my habit of taking on too many roles and not delegating effectively. When faced with the possibility of another employee OR manager leaving, I knew I couldn't handle taking on additional duties. It was time to stop wearing multiple hats, let go, and move forward. And so, I resigned. The metamorphosis had begun, and I was ready to emerge as my new self, or at least figure out what my new self might be. I didn't have a clue

One week after leaving my job, I got a dog—something I had postponed for years due to my long working hours. Like many others during Covid, we bought an RV to continue traveling. Engaging in activities I truly enjoyed, I experienced genuine liberation from the constraints of a nine-to-five job. For the first time in twenty-four years as a nurse, I prioritized self-care to recharge and reflect on what my future path was going to be.

Over the next year, we built a community with friends and neighbors, forming a biking club called the Go-Go Gang. We cycled, trained, ran, and spent time supporting each other in our performance goals. Toward the end of 2021, one year after leaving my job, I decided to run a half marathon. My neighbors showed me the power of community—how much easier it is to work toward goals with the support of others. I completed the 3M half marathon, which had a big impact on me. I started to believe in myself again, feeling I could accomplish anything I set my heart and mind to.

Buoyed by this newfound confidence and further encouragement from the Go-Go Gang, I set my sights on a triathlon. That goal seemed insurmountable because I wasn't a swimmer. However, with renewed ambition, I believed I could learn. I had always been a water person, enjoying cooling off in pools and lakes during the Texas heat. So, I learned to swim, joined a master's swim class at the YMCA, and trained diligently for a triathlon. In the fall of 2022, I completed the Kerrville Sprint

Triathlon. I was elated—it felt incredible to achieve such significant goals!

I enjoyed feeling physically fit and strong. I realized having a strong body creates a strong spirit, which supports a strong mind. I was experiencing holistic health, which allowed me to have clearer thoughts, goals, and dreams. I had reduced stress, and I was free from anxiety. As a result, I began sensing a tug toward finding a purposeful career again. Taking a year off from my career to focus on health and wellness had a big impact on me. Although I still found myself processing past experiences, healing was evident.

Looking back on my career, I started to feel proud of my accomplishments rather than discouraged. I often woke up from dreams of walking the halls of the operating room, speaking with staff, and panicking about forgetting something important. These dreams were my mind's way of processing and releasing my past, preparing me to embrace the next chapter of my life.

My varied nursing experiences have provided me with invaluable knowledge and skills. This background gave me confidence in my abilities, laying a strong foundation for eventually starting my own clinic once I had healed and discovered my next purpose in life.

When considering my next career moves, I proceeded cautiously. I created an LLC and began renting out the RV we purchased during the height of Covid. Even though the world had started recovering, people still preferred camping to international travel. Our little camper, nicknamed Sunshine Bear, was rented out every weekend throughout the summer of 2022 and occasionally into the fall.

I was slowly re-entering the workforce, but after that first summer, I realized renting just one RV wasn't enough for a profitable business. Scaling up to a fleet of RVs seemed necessary to utilize time and resources effectively. Given the high demand for camping during Covid, I even considered starting an all-inclusive RV resort. Ultimately, I concluded that I wasn't passionate enough about RVs to pursue it further.

Through community and self-care, my heart reopened to hope and purpose. I considered nursing again, but struggled with what that might look like. I couldn't envision returning to a traditional nursing job, especially after experiencing the chaos of the pandemic. Working in an allopathic setting no longer resonated with me, and I couldn't imagine stepping back into any of my previous roles.

I didn't want to return to a lifestyle marked by overwork, which compromised my health and family life. My values had shifted, I was now focused on nurturing my body, mind, and spirit, committed to living holistically.

I genuinely felt that God was guiding me along this path. Each time I chose a new direction, the next steps appeared effortlessly, affirming that I was exactly where I was meant to be.

I searched for new opportunities online and saw a posting for an IV nutrition nurse. I sent a message expressing my interest, marking the start of a transformative career shift. When I met with the person who posted the position, I immediately knew it was the next step. My transformation was underway.

Within a short period, I learned the myths and truths about nutrition and our food system. I discovered that our bodies function as systems requiring balance and that environmental toxins and preservatives in food contribute significantly to many common diseases today.

As a nurse at detoxification retreats, I started IV infusions of vitamin mixtures administered over several hours. Clients began their day with smoothies made from homemade almond milk and organic fruit, accompanied by various tinctures and capsules designed for detoxification.

During treatment sessions, clients watched films featuring farmers growing organic produce and ranchers raising animals humanely. Available therapies included PEMF, IV nutrition, nasal hydrogen, and high-dose ozone IV. Lectures were presented on healthy food choices and foods to avoid. Lunch typically consisted of another smoothie, bone broth, and additional detox supplements. As clients received treatments, I learned alongside them, gaining valuable insight into making healthier choices.

Many clients came to detox treatment cycles feeling relieved to have someone listen to their concerns. Often, they'd already visited numerous doctors and been prescribed medications that weren't helping. When they voiced their concerns to these doctors, they'd hear dismissive comments like, "There's nothing wrong with you," or, "It's all in your head."

Often, clients have shared stories of being diagnosed with chronic illnesses, prescribed lifelong medications, and being told this was their new reality. Many refused to accept this as the final truth and chose not to take the prescribed medications. Through their research, they discovered alternative therapies like ozone therapy, nutrition, and other holistic treatments. When these clients arrive for detox treatments, they come filled with hope that there's another path to wellness beyond what they've been previously told.

Unfortunately, the current healthcare system has significant gaps. Take cancer treatment as an example. Chemotherapy is given to eliminate cancer cells, yet it is widely known to compromise the immune system severely. Thus, a patient who already has a weakened immune system, contributing to the cancer's development, undergoes chemotherapy, further weakening their immune response.

If the cancer goes into remission, it's considered a success, and the patient is declared "cancer-free" and released from oncology care. However, no guidance or support is typically provided afterward to rebuild their severely compromised immune system. This gap leaves a substantial need for immune system support, yet no conventional solutions are offered post-treatment.

This is precisely where ozone therapy bridges the gap. Regardless of where an individual is in their health journey, ozone therapy helps restore cellular function and balance. It boosts the immune system, detoxifies the body, destroys harmful microorganisms, and revitalizes energy production within the mitochondria of cells.

Ozone therapy is also highly beneficial for autoimmune disorders, circulatory conditions, Lyme disease, viral and bacterial infections, skin issues, respiratory illnesses, heavy metal toxicity, joint pain, inflammatory conditions, and other diseases caused by toxin accumulation. Additionally, ozone therapy is excellent for individuals seeking optimal health in today's toxin-filled environment.

Within six months, I learned more about diet, nutrition, and alternative therapies than I'd acquired in my entire life. Witnessing firsthand how these treatments improved individual health was incredibly eye-opening. Many of these therapies were new to me, but one particularly captured my interest—high-dose ozone therapy.

High-dose ozone therapy effectively detoxifies, stimulates cellular repair, and kills microorganisms better than any other treatment I've encountered. In the fall of 2022, I attended a training conference led by Dr. Frank Shallenberger. Dr. Shallenberger, who graduated medical school in 1973, initially practiced conventional medicine but soon recognized that merely managing symptoms with medications wasn't beneficial enough for his patients. He sought alternative approaches, including ozone therapy.

The knowledge gained at the Nevada conference and witnessing clients' profound healing at monthly detox retreats completely redirected my career path.

I knew I needed to shift from monthly treatment cycles to something more consistent. While searching again for IV nutrition opportunities, I connected with someone planning to open an IV nutrition clinic within a med spa. Although this wasn't my long-term goal, I seized the opportunity to learn about operating an IV clinic. It also gave me valuable insights into running a med spa business—an excellent model for setting up my future ozone clinic.

While I enjoyed my work there, my passion bubbled beneath the surface: helping others through ozone therapy. Unfortunately, no clinics offered specialized high-dose ozone therapy near me. It had been six months since my last experience with ozone treatments at the detox retreats, and I missed witnessing the incredible benefits clients received.

At that point, I had a stark realization: entrepreneurs find the resources to start their ventures while employees wait for someone else to provide opportunities. I was beyond the employee mindset. Feeling trapped by not performing the therapies I loved, I committed to finding the resources to invest in ozone equipment.

My vision was clear. I wanted to guide people toward healthy lifestyles, proper nutrition, and transformative therapies, incorporating my core values of God, family, and wellness. I ordered a specialized ozone machine from Germany for high-dose ozone therapy. Since the machine would take several months to pass customs and arrive, I sought a suitable clinic location.

Within a week of reaching out to my community, I was connected with a realtor who had a clean, bright, and affordable space, offering both private and shared areas— perfect for launching my clinic.

In July 2023, the ozone machine finally arrived, and my Ozone clinic, NaturO3, officially opened its doors. The community I'd connected with at my first detox and wellness job became my very first clients. They continued encouraging me and showed incredible support from the start.

Just after opening the doors to NaturO3 Ozone Clinic, I accepted an invitation to a networking event with a focus on branding for businesses. The speaker was a portrait photographer and mindset coach. I learned incredible insights about how to brand, market, network and grow a business.

From that experience, I signed up for my first ever professional headshot and made valuable connections that were the spark for building my networking community. Those connections have grown into an abundant network of business owners and wellness providers for collaboration.

As a result, in addition to offering wellness therapies, the first year of the clinic's operation was filled with meetings, lunches, groups, events, and countless connections. Networking and community-building became a foundation of the clinic in order to grow organically. When invited by someone to an event or to visit a group, I consider them all. I never know what connection might be at the next event that could move the collaboration gauge in a positive way.

I have a business coach who shared a valuable insight with me. As an individual, I can achieve a great deal, but through collaboration, we can accomplish even more. This idea is echoed in the African proverb: If you want to go fast, go alone. If you want to go far, go together.

I developed personal mottos that supported my mindset as a business owner. One key philosophy I embraced is, "You've got to show up to grow up." This motto carries multiple meanings, but for me, it meant stepping out of my comfort zone and actively participating in events I was invited to.

Equally important was releasing expectations. Typically, a single event doesn't immediately lead to new clients; however, repeatedly seeing someone at multiple events builds trust, allowing connections to form naturally and authentically rather than feeling forced. I attended numerous networking events, and I still do!

Another guiding principle is, if you're comfortable, you're not growing. During my first year in business, I felt like I grew to 100 feet tall. Whenever I felt particularly uncomfortable, I reminded myself that discomfort signaled growth. Knowing there was still much growth ahead, I enthusiastically embraced those challenges.

A third set of principles originated from my upbringing and have guided me throughout my life, becoming even more relevant in business: "If you're going to do it, do it right," and "Always do the right thing." Adhering to these principles can sometimes be challenging. Doing things correctly can be more time-consuming, costly, or demanding. However, consistently following these mottos provides peace of mind and demonstrates integrity to others.

The first year of opening Naturo3 was a whirlwind of learning, attending events, self-reflection, onboarding new clients, and educating others about ozone therapy. My vision continued to take shape, and long-term growth goals evolved. During this first year, the business experienced strong organic growth, and I developed significantly as a business owner. Most obstacles I faced were due to my decisions, emphasizing the importance of a constant thirst for knowledge and adaptability. If something wasn't working, I learned to address it promptly and adjust accordingly.

As the first anniversary of Naturo3 approached, I was outside my original lease terms but continuing with month-to-month payments. While contemplating moving to a larger and more modern space, I realized I'd become somewhat complacent, considering options without taking action. However, it seemed God had different plans. Suddenly, the landlord sold our part of the building, and new tenants quickly moved into the shared area outside the clinic door. Within just 24 hours, the space became overcrowded.

Instead of feeling upset or complaining, I saw this situation as a clear sign; it was time to move and grow. Prompted by urgency, I immediately began searching for new locations. As before, one lead led to another, guiding me forward. While driving around, I noticed a beautiful suite with a "for rent" sign. I called immediately and secured the space the very next day. Within a week, we had moved. I viewed everything that occurred as a blessing, confident that God was guiding me toward the perfect space for continued growth.

In 2022, when I embarked on the journey to discover my future direction, I felt that I needed the presence of the Lord with me more than I ever had. Perhaps because big dreams and goals come with equally big obstacles and hurdles.

Exhaustion, brain fog, fear, or doubt can make a goal seem far away. In these times, I put my faith in God that I can overcome obstacles, if it is his will, often choosing faith over fear. If a goal seems to move away, I pray for the strength to complete the tasks in order to make it happen. If it isn't working, I ask for his guidance to choose another path. It might be necessary to walk away, pray, or just wait.

At times, I would feel uneasy about not having enough clients or a slow clinic schedule. Instead of spending energy worrying, I would use the time to work on another project and focus on something else. Often, within a few hours, a client would reach out for services. These experiences continually reassured me that God works in His time, not mine, reinforcing the importance of trusting fully in Him.

Today, I'm excited to live my purpose daily by offering clients at Naturo3 Ozone Clinic therapies that bridge the gaps in healthcare, provide hope for better health outcomes, and foster a community that listens to and acknowledges the ongoing challenges of chronic illnesses and health struggles.

In my practice, I see people regain energy, experience pain relief, and feel *alive* again. I watch immune systems rebuild, chronic infections fade, and inflammation subside. I am not just running a business—I am fulfilling a mission. I had once believed my nursing career was over. Instead, I have found a way to heal people more deeply than ever. Every day, I meet people desperate for answers. They have been dismissed, misdiagnosed, or left without solutions. They come in tired and defeated.

I believe in bridging the gaps in healthcare, restoring the body's ability to heal, and giving people the tools they need to truly feel well again. Regular detoxification is vital for maintaining healthy cellular function. The therapies we offer provide detoxification, immune modulation, improved cellular function, circulation, and oxygenation. Working on these processes in the body helps bring the cells of the body back to balance, allowing the body to heal itself, the way God intended. Our clinic's motto encapsulates this process perfectly. Detox. Recover. Repair. Repeat.

Today, I am excited to live my purpose. NaturO3 is more than a clinic. It's a place for healing. A place for hope. A place for those who refuse to give up on their health. And I wouldn't trade it for anything.

If there's one lesson I've learned, it's that purpose is not a single destination—it's a journey. I had spent so much of my life chasing goals, believing that success was measured by achievement. But the truth is, the journey itself is where life happens.

Why do we push ourselves to the breaking point, living out of balance? Why do we believe that worth comes only from doing more, achieving more, *being* more? Maybe it's ego, perhaps it's our culture, maybe it's a lack of trust in God's timing. But I know now that slowing down, listening, and being still allows clarity to emerge. And when we quiet the noise, we can finally hear the truth of who we are meant to be.

For me, that truth had been there all along: helping others, serving with compassion, and finding ways to bring healing, not just through medicine, but through human connection. That realization set the stage for the next chapter of my life, one in which healing goes beyond nursing and conventional medicine into a new world of holistic wellness.

It all started with a little girl pushing a wheelchair, eager to make someone smile, and it never stopped.

SHELLEY LARSEN

Shelley Larsen, BSN, is a registered nurse with twenty-five years of experience. With an unwavering commitment to improving people's lives, she saw a gap in the healthcare system that left patients without wellness. Shelley searched for therapies that did more than manage symptoms. Upon research she discovered natural and holistic therapies including ozone.

This discovery led her to open Naturo3 Ozone Clinic. The clinic focuses on nutrition, cutting-edge therapies in ozone, longevity and biohacking to create a modern space of healing and hope.

Her passion is to educate, collaborate and create a community of like-minded individuals who want a healthier way of life for themselves and their families.

Her goal is to open several locations of Naturo3 Ozone Clinic in the Central Texas area in order to improve health with nutrition and therapies that detoxify, recover, and repair the body.

Shelley enjoys reading, the farmer's market, listening to podcasts, cooking and spending time with her family. She is an author of the book *Boat Burning for Beginners* and is excited to share holistic health with others.

Learn about Naturo3: www.naturo3.com
LinkedIn: shelleylarsen
Facebook: https://www.facebook.com/
shelleygilmorelarsen
Facebook: Naturo3
Instagram: @naturo3.tx

7

BOBBING AND WEAVING: THE ART OF ADAPTABILITY

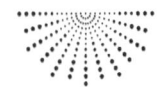

BY JANNA PAULSON

When my phone rings, I answer after the first ring. In my business, timing is everything.

"The client wants to push the install date again," my procurement team advises. This is the seventh time it has been pushed.

"Okay, let's see what everyone's availability is," I say.

Karina confirms, "The office furniture vendor and the game table supplier can make the new date; however, the custom banquette manufacturer needs to deliver either a week before or two weeks later. What do you want me to do?"

I explain I need to email our client to relay the details and ask if construction is okay with the banquette being delivered early. The usual back-and-forth of rescheduling and confirming continues all day until everything finally gels.

My day typically starts by quickly assessing, adjusting, and coordinating. If I'm lucky and everyone is agreeable, I bob and weave my way to another victory.

On install day, I leave Austin early in the morning to arrive in Houston in time to meet the warehouse team. They've already arrived and are unloading the truck. Hundreds of boxes are strewn across the driveway. Workers are everywhere—opening boxes, moving furniture, assembling pieces, and asking questions.

The amenity area is stunning. As I walk in, I take in the lighting, decorative tile, custom desk, and overall feel of the space. It's awe-inspiring. Before I can put my things down, Jose is already asking, "Miss Janna—this came in damaged. I need you to look at this." Another worker shouts, "Miss Janna—where does this go?" And then, "Miss Janna, Miss Janna...." It goes on and on as I pivot in every direction, trying to answer each question. If only they would glance at the presentation on the table showing each item's placement, but they defer to asking me.

The process involves constant movement—in front of the building, down the hall, and outside by the pool. We don't stop until the building is completely furnished, usually eight hours later. There is no lunch break, and there is no time to check emails. My son calls, and I tell him, "Honey, I'm on an install. I can't talk."

There's a sense of calm and quiet when everything is finally in place. The big "TA-DA" moment. This is the best part of the process—seeing all the creative elements come together. It's beautiful and rewarding. Everyone has left, and I am the only one in the building. I tour the property, admiring the sofa, the art, the composition, and the overall feeling of the space.

I created this.

Wow. Or, as my stepfather would say, "Holy cow."

It takes years to complete, but it is so worth it. This is what keeps me coming back.

There is so much more to design than just the "look". Being an Interior Designer requires more technical knowledge than most people realize. We coordinate work with Architects, MEP (mechanical, electrical, and plumbing) Engineers, Structural Engineers, and AV consultants. Our drawings must integrate with theirs so the construction team understands the full scope of work.

Often, something is overlooked. For example, the MEP team might not include our floor cores or decorative lighting or design general illumination without considering our ceiling details. Multiple reviews will hopefully catch these issues early.

Last month, we installed a project in Houston with two powered conference tables. Upon arrival, we noticed that construction had not followed our drawings—no outlets. I notified our client and asked how they wanted to proceed. They chose the correct answer: make construction go back and fix it. I love it when that happens.

What we do is fluid. You cannot be rigid and succeed in this field—it's all about give and take. There are just too many variables.

Bobbing and weaving come naturally to me, but as the third child of four, I learned early to come out swinging to protect my territory.

In elementary school, I had a beautiful gold dress that I loved, and I wore it frequently. Unfortunately, a boy decided to tease me, calling me "Cinderella, Cinderella." I didn't like that, so I pushed him down. The teasing continued into middle school, "Janna Banana, Janna Banana." I would run, hide, and cry. Did I mention I was a scrawny, towheaded blonde girl?

In high school, female athletes didn't like me because I displaced one of their friends on the team or because I dressed differently. I was a novelty for a brief period, then discarded. I spent many lunches in the library to avoid the embarrassment of sitting alone. Being an underdog gave me the grit and determination to excel at sports, and later, in business.

At the same time, my parents divorced. I attended two elementary, two middle, and three high schools. My mother married three times, and my father married four times. My siblings and I—each born one year apart—were shuttled back and forth from San Antonio to Austin, Paradise Valley to Austin, and Tempe to Austin.

Adaptability was learned at an early age. And that experience contributed to my success.

It's hard to believe, but yes, perseverance builds character. To persevere, you must be adaptable and find different ways to forge ahead.

My mother's household was calm and stable compared to my father's.

"You kids do whatever you want, but pick your friends wisely," he'd say. He always emphasized thinking positively: "Positive things happen to positive people."

I didn't always have the luxury of stability, so I learned to adapt.

At the same time, both of my parents encouraged me to believe I could do anything. My aspirations were unlimited.

That's not to say everything was smooth and finding the right path wasn't immediate.

With a father, Larry Peel, immersed in multifamily development, weekends often meant tagging along to construction sites, critiquing details, and discussing solutions. Summer jobs transformed from sweeping floors to cleaning pools to working in leasing offices—each role was a lesson in engaging with residents and construction crews.

My father allowed me to sit in his meetings with the Architect and Interior Designer. At this time, I was majoring in Architecture, and learning on the job was an incredible opportunity.

Creativity runs in the family. My stepfather, Leonard Lehrer, an international artist and head of ASU's Fine Arts Program, ensured lifelong exposure to artistic processes and international travel. Encouragement was never in short supply.

Two years into the School of Architecture, the reality of an extended graduation timeline prompted a shift to graphic design. Yet, the lack of technology in the '80s made hand-drawing every element painstaking. Finally, a landing—interior design—where everything clicked.

Changing direction isn't failure; it's clarity. The moment of truth came with the decision to drop accounting. Bracing for disapproval, my mother responded: "Okay."

Relief. I could now pursue my passion without fear, even if it meant five years to graduate.

Even before college, hard work started early. A paper route in middle school. The ice cream station at Organ

Stop Pizza was a favorite post—until a sister's breakup with the manager led to an untimely firing. High school introduced an accounting office job at a lumber company. College meant hostessing at El Torito and Who Song & Larry's, eventually working up to back-office roles. Accomplishing tasks fueled motivation. If something needed doing, it got done. That drive became an essential trait in business ownership.

Returning to Austin post-graduation led to a position at a Houston-based architecture firm with a small Austin satellite office. The firm dominated the space-planning market for newly built office buildings in the early eighties, including Michael Dell's first office space. Only four or five firms provided the same service. We were hired to space plan space for most of the new office buildings built that decade. We grew cocky and overconfident as we had the lion's share of work.

My confidence soared, and work was abundant. Yet, creativity remained limited within strict construction drawings.

A job shift brought the long-awaited blend of design and space planning. Seeing what we could create—restaurants, radio stations, law firms—was liberating and exhilarating. Finally, the pieces came together.

By 1989, Austin's economy was suffering. Work slowed, and the office stayed uncomfortably slow. Rather than sit still, I filled time with cleaning windows and reorganizing the library—anything to keep busy. The thought of taking a salary while doing nothing felt unbearable.

Fresh off passing the National Council of Interior Design Qualification (NCIDQ) exam, I decided to start my own business. My relationships with commercial real estate brokers provided a crucial launching point. All it took was one solid client.

Office buildings became my niche. When tenants showed interest, a meeting was scheduled, and I would design a schematic of their space. I thrived when meeting new people and dealing with the challenges that come with nearly every project.

Contract work with a former boss supplemented income while building momentum. Then, the moment arrived when I could go full-time on my own.

Controlling my destiny was exhilarating. Owning a business meant working as much and as hard as desired —every day, all day. The pace never slowed. Each completed project was a stepping stone to the next, and I learned even more about how to bob and weave.

As I ventured into entrepreneurship, realistic goals were essential. Aiming high is important, but keeping overhead low is crucial; a former boss drilled that lesson into me. Fear-driven decisions lead nowhere, and I became strategic in my relationships.

Opportunities rarely knock on their own. Sometimes, the front door isn't the way in, maybe it's a side door. Success demanded putting myself out there, networking strategically, and being involved in the community. Professional organizations, industry connections, and a passion for the work separate me from many competitors. Ethics stand at the core. How a problem is handled sets me apart. Taking the high road and finding solutions have helped me create long-term success. With a passion for making my clients' lives easier, I make myself indispensable.

My work is my life. Business doesn't stop at the office door. It lingers, follows me home, and even seeps into dreams. Some of the best processing happens while I'm sleeping. Weekends provide uninterrupted time to get ahead. Risk and reward walk hand in hand—failure is always possible, but so is a reward if I've learned from my mistakes and made the necessary changes.

Hiring the first employee after one year in business marked a turning point. Growth brought challenges, particularly in management. My first significant mistake was treating employees as tools, assigning tasks rather than fostering development. In the early days, I cherry-picked projects while passing off the less desirable ones.

Another lesson came hard and fast when a first solo client meeting resulted in being steamrolled. Clients weren't interested in answering questions; they wanted to tell their stories.

Listening became the strategy. Let the client speak first. Once their thoughts were out, circling back with necessary questions became easier. Conversations became collaborative, and clients felt heard.

A recent book I read by Will Guidara called *Unreasonable Hospitality* reinforced this approach. The author emphasized not "sucking the air out of the room." People engage more when they feel ownership in the process.

Three years in, another economic downturn arrived. Watching employees look for reassurance while personally navigating uncertainty was agonizing. Sitting in the Cushman & Wakefield office, asking brokers about potential projects, became routine. Agility was the only way forward. Shifting from corporate office work to government contracts kept the business afloat. We worked with the Texas Natural Resource Conservation Commission and the Workers' Compensation Commission.

Being adaptable extended our lifeline and taught us some new skills. Back then, I was still drafting ink on mylar. One large client had a very tight schedule and expected me to complete a full floor of construction drawings every day.

That included the partition plan, electrical plan, lighting plan, and any millwork elevations. I knew I needed help, so I asked an architect specializing in dental offices to assist. We worked until midnight or later, whatever was necessary, to meet our deadlines. That was the grind. That's what was expected.

It wasn't unusual for me to be brought into a conference room, handed a programming booklet, and asked to complete a schematic design that same day. The real estate market was fiercely competitive; the quicker you could turn something around, the better the broker's chance of closing the deal. It was stressful. Interior designers ranked just above the construction team in the pecking order.

My husband will tell you I hand-picked him out of the room, which I did. I was at an Italian restaurant called Mezzaluna and saw him across the room. I knew the people he was with and asked one to come over. This guy thought I was hitting on him, but no, I wanted an introduction to Steve. That is all she wrote, as they say.

Marriage changed the rhythm of work, and having a child transformed priorities altogether, changing the entire outlook on the type of work we did. Nicholas was born ten years into my business. Those "churn and burn" deadlines lost their appeal. Don't get me wrong—I continued working through the next bust cycle—but I began craving something more meaningful and eventually transitioned into multifamily design.

I loved being a mom. My son was a ray of sunshine, and I took him everywhere. He attended design fundraisers and ran backstage at the Paramount Theater when we redesigned the chorus rooms—basically, wherever I went, he followed. I admit I'm guilty of putting him first. Back then, it was difficult to prioritize who or what came first —my husband, my business, or my son. Most of you know that your business almost always ends up numero uno. I still struggle with this. There's a constant push-pull of compromises when trying to make everyone happy.

My son's middle and high school years brought some of the most challenging moments in life—knees-to-the-ground, crying moments. Parenthood, like business, requires constant adaptation. You can't force a child—or a project—to be something it's not. You adjust. You shift. You find a way forward. But survival, perseverance, and love prevailed. Today, Nicholas is preparing to graduate from college, and the house is an empty nest.

Decades of industry involvement have created strong relationships. As a founding member of the International Interior Designers Association, I have served as chapter president, regional director—covering Louisiana, Mississippi, Oklahoma, and Texas—and residential forum advisor on the International Board—

twenty years of active participation in helping shape the interior design industry.

Beyond design, community engagement shaped my journey—sixteen years on the Paramount Theatre Board, six years on the Texas Book Festival Board (five of those as gala chair), three years on the Texas Women for the Arts Board, and current service on the BUILT Austin Executive Board. Giving back and community service were core values instilled by my father: If you can, do. As a natural connector with people, I love learning about what makes them tick.

An idea I had recently led to a principals' roundtable where I brought fifteen interior design firms together to discuss industry challenges. Leading the initiative alongside the Texas Association of Interior Designers, the goal was clear—protecting the profession from legislative threats.

During the legislative session every two years, someone tries to remove our licensing or tax our services. A license allows me to stamp drawings for building permits, a game-changer for someone who owns their own firm. Without this license, drawings would have to be stamped by an architect. TAID hires a lobbyist to watch for any red flags that need addressing during the session. With a very small committee to drive this organization and raise money, I jumped right in. We thought holding an event would be a good way to spread the word to other designers and firms.

Fifteen firms were represented, and as each person introduced themselves, stating how many years they'd practiced and lived in Austin, I felt a bit humbled. The group included the world's largest architectural firm, Gensler, along with Perkins and Will, Page, IA, and others. Most attendees had been practicing for around twenty years. When it was my turn to introduce myself, I proudly announced my business was thirty-six years old, and I had practiced for forty years. I felt proud but also a little old.

I'm always nervous in groups like this, feeling insecure about not being part of a larger firm. Many attendees have no idea who I am, as most have only recently moved to Austin, whereas I grew up here.

After a brief social period, we broke into small groups at separate tables to discuss assigned topics. My group included an educator from Texas State, two people from large corporate firms, and someone from a boutique rockstar architecture firm. We discussed students entering the workforce, Gen Z's "all about me" approach, and company perks.

Listening to how structured and rigid the large firms were made me feel justified in running my smaller firm the way I chose. I couldn't believe some firms allowed designers only eight hours for representative meetings or educational classes. We are far more flexible. If an opportunity arises, we seize it. I've taken my designers to the Stockholm Furniture Fair, Salone del Mobile in Milan, and Light + Build in Frankfurt. We attend all major U.S. shows and markets—Neocon, Hospitality Design, the International Contemporary Furniture Fair, and Boutique Design New York. I believe the more exposure someone has to the world, the better educated and creatively broad they become.

Over my many years in business, I've learned how not to overreact or "sweat the small stuff." My staff looks to me for support, patience, mentorship, fairness, and strength. The art of getting things done draws a clear line. The office tone is set by its people's energy, grace, and style. People are people; we all need to be heard. Not just the employees but also the clients and vendors who work with us. Patience and kindness are essential. It doesn't have to be purely transactional; it can be enriching and fulfilling.

Today, I'm much more in tune with my staff than I was at the beginning. We're a team, and I support them. I strive to remove stress from their lives, caring for them and nurturing their growth as they mature professionally. In some ways, I'm their surrogate mother. They know they can always come to me, and I'll handle the difficult client or situation. Nothing brings me more joy than a happy client or a beautiful space.

My growth plan is to become more involved with national organizations to broaden our reach into different states. PPDS has grown beyond Texas, with work spanning Arizona, Colorado, Florida, Mississippi, New Mexico, and North Carolina. The goal is national recognition of my company as a leader in multifamily interior design, where creativity, skill, and collaboration set the standard.

My industry is constantly evolving, and to survive as a small business owner, you must adapt. When I think of where I began to where I am now, it wouldn't have been possible without that agility. In design, we are always tweaking things. Business is the same.

Why do I love this work? I love the challenge. I love watching young designers grow and expand their talents and confidence. I love hearing clients praise our work. It's rewarding to see our name on projects and to have people say, "Oh, you're Janna Paulson, the talented interior designer—I've heard of you!" The name recognition feels good, and the legacy I'm leaving feels even better.

JANNA PAULSON

Janna Paulson, RID, LEED AP, WELL AP is the founding member of Peel Paulson Design Studio and manages three office locations, Austin, Denver, and San Antonio. Her forty years of interior design experience include corporate, retail, government, hospitality, residential and multifamily clientele. Having grown up in the industry, she followed in her father's (Larry Peel) footsteps.

She understands all phases of the design process and focuses on a creative streamlined approach collaborating with the development team. Janna's strong relationship with manufacturers allows her to bring a better product and pricing to her clients. She regularly attends various industry markets including Neocon, ICFF, HD, Las Vegas as well as Light + Build, Salone de Milano and the Stockholm Furniture Fair. PPDS work can be found in Arizona, Colorado, Florida, Georgia, New Mexico, North Carolina and Texas.

Mrs Paulson graduated from Arizona State University and studied abroad in Florence, Italy. She devoted her early years to the design industry serving in leadership roles with ASID & IIDA. She is active in her local community serving on the Paramount Theatre's Presidents Council, Texas Book Festival Board of Directors and The Texas Cultural Trust Texas Women for the Arts. When she has free time, Janna plays golf, travels and researches great restaurants.

Instagram PPDS: @ppds_design
Facebook PPDS: http://facebook.com/PPDSdesign/
LinkedIn: janna-paulson-13a85b14
LinkedIn PPDS: company/ppds

8

THE ACCIDENTAL ENTREPRENEUR

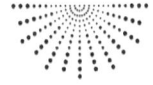

BY JAMIE MATUSEK

I sat at the red light watching the rain pour down the windshield. It was the kind of night when the cold seeped deep into your bones. Not a soul was behind me. I glanced in the rearview mirror, watching the red taillights of cars passing by me disappear in the downpour, and wondered, *Where are they going?*

Tears streamed down my cheeks, mirroring the rain cascading down the glass. The weight of loneliness settled in, and the "what ifs" hit.

What if I missed my opportunities? What if my choices lead to a dead end? What if I always live in lack? What if I never step into the dreams buried deep in my heart?

Then, the light turned green. I pressed my foot against the gas pedal, and in that instant, something clicked. I was done believing that my dreams were out of reach, done letting fear dictate my direction. That moment was a turning point, though I could never have imagined the winding, treacherous, beautiful journey ahead.

This "red light moment" was the first of many times that I would face a challenge and be presented with the choice to stay stuck at the proverbial light or take a risk and put my foot on the gas to move ahead. One of the biggest red light moments came when I decided to step into entrepreneurship. The challenge was presented, the fear crept in, and my foot hovered above the gas pedal.

Entrepreneurship wasn't part of my plan. I envisioned myself working for someone else, climbing the corporate ladder, rebuilding teams, and fixing broken systems—turning broken things into something beautiful. I wanted the stability of an organization's security. A stable paycheck. A roadmap to retirement.

I was an intreprenuer expert! This is a level of employment when you reach the C-Suite, and it offers many opportunities of entrepreneurship, like more autonomy, but with the security of a steady paycheck. You can invent, build, and grow without carrying all of the risk of a business owner.

That was my plan with a capital P. [Insert the LOL here.] As Proverbs 19:21 says, "Many are the plans in a person's heart, but it is the Lord's purpose that prevails." That truth unraveled everything I thought I wanted.

Small-Town Roots, Big-City Dreams

Moving to the big city was the first leap or red light moment. I grew up in a small town in Southeast Texas called Palacios. Country living was my life. My dad was a shrimper (yes, like Forrest Gump) and owned a grass farm. My mom was a stay-at-home mom before returning to school to become a teacher. Hard work was our foundation. On any given day, you'd find me shucking corn, moving water pipe, or heading out with my dad on the shrimp boat lovingly named "Miss Jamie."

But I had bigger dreams. I wanted to see the world beyond our tiny town. I looked forward to spreading my wings and experiencing college life in the city. I started college at Texas State before transferring to Texas A&M to be with the love of my life. College was a shock, but I adapted, graduated, and packed up for Dallas with all the confidence of someone who had never yet faced failure. Like Wonder Woman, I was ready to take on the world.

My first job at a marketing agency placed me at a six-foot folding table in a hallway, my executive seat, as I liked to call it. The view was of downtown, and I imagined I had made it in the big city.

I showed up in hand-sewn suits, ribbons still in my hair, unaware of what lay ahead. Thankfully, my coworkers made me feel like a movie star when they cleared out my closets, took me shopping, and scheduled a makeover.

The first copy I submitted returned so marked up that it looked like my boss had pricked his finger and bled all over it. My first client call ended with the client advising me to take speaking classes to lose my Texas twang.

Still, I loved it. I thrived under pressure, learned to manage high-profile clients, and figured out how to navigate office politics. I worked harder, climbed higher, and never stopped to ask if I was on the right path.

Then I saw it; a salary list left at the copy machine. My name was near the top, but below it was the name of a man, several years my junior, who reported to me, and he was making significantly more.

That was my first real lesson: hard work doesn't automatically equal recognition.

I didn't pause to consider my worth. I didn't ask myself, *Am I being valued here? Is this where I want to grow?* Instead, I got to work. I built a case for my raise, prepared presentations, and negotiated my worth. But I never stopped moving, never took a moment to reflect.

Then, September eleventh happened. The world shifted overnight, and suddenly, marketing jobs dried up. The agency held on to as many team members as long as possible, but layoffs became inevitable. I was lucky—I stayed employed. I navigated layoffs, uncertainty, and the responsibility of leading my team through a crisis. The girl from the shrimp boat had become a woman who stood her ground in the face of adversity.

My team looked to me for answers and encouragement, and I showed up to do just that. Then, I cried at home. I leveled up from a shy country girl to a woman who showed courage, perseverance, and resiliency. Even in the face of fear and the unknown, I kept moving forward. This formed the first foundational pieces of leadership.

But as I watched my colleagues pack up their desks, I wondered for the first time: *What happens when your planned path disappears?*

Moving, Marriage, and Missteps

Before September eleventh, my husband and I had planned a move from Dallas to Austin. I had multiple job interviews and offers on the table, but after that disastrous day, marketing opportunities dried up. The job hunt was brutal. I found a remote role with a small Dallas agency, but didn't ask the right questions. Before I knew it, they lost two key accounts and couldn't pay me. There was no severance, no warning, just a "Goodbye and good luck."

I was terrified. And I didn't pause. I just kept moving.

Desperate for work, I ended up selling cars. A marketing professional turned car salesperson. Round peg. Square hole. It was humbling. But it led to something unexpected—a connection with a family-owned business that saw something in me. Within a week, I had an offer. It was thirty-thousand dollars less than I had made in Dallas, but it was an opportunity.

Did I pause and evaluate whether this was the right fit? No. I just jumped in.

For the next seven years, I led sales and marketing efforts, managed a company rebrand, and helped launch one of the first direct mail mobile apps. I had my son, learned to balance motherhood and career, and kept climbing. I experienced what it was like to be pregnant in a workplace, go on maternity leave, and then navigate being a breastfeeding working mom leading a team.

I can't say I remember those first few months due to sleep deprivation, but I made it. I leveled up again. I learned new skills and experienced entirely different industries, including real estate, franchise organizations, remodeling and building companies, and so much more. It led to expanded confidence. Once again, I added another layer to the foundation of leadership and built courage, perseverance, and resilience.

But I never asked myself, *Am I happy here? Do I see a future in this?*

Then, life unraveled: divorce, single motherhood, and financial strain. I needed a change, so I took the first job that offered me stability and a challenge: a fitness start-up. There, I built processes, managed a team, and navigated the fast-paced world of direct-to-consumer sales. Going client-side always intrigued me. What would it be like to sit in that seat? I was getting my chance.

The role took me on new adventures into television advertising, messaging, and marketing to sell equipment. It was my first exposure to a direct-to-consumer call center and influencer marketing, and it was exciting and fun. I loved the people and the work, but like with many start-ups, the budget shifted dramatically. After a year, I heard a similar story right before Christmas: "We don't have the money to support your role anymore."

This was another moment when I should have paused, assessed, and planned. But I didn't.

Panic set in. Single mom. No income. No plan.

"Lord, if you hear me, please help me."

My phone rang before I pulled into my driveway after being let go. My former boss needed help. "How soon can you throw on a suit and get over here for an interview?" What? These things don't just happen, do they? I ran inside, wiped the tears away, threw on my makeup and that fancy suit, and hit the road. Another shake. Another shift. Another move. Another level-up.

I didn't stop to ask, "Is this the right role for me?"

When I stepped in the door, my boss laid out the task. I was to transform an in-house team into a stand-alone, successful operation. My task was to look at everything, including operational infrastructure, service offerings, pricing, client mix, team culture, and talent. Oh, and by the way, work to overcome a broken and toxic working environment with the parent company. It was my specialty! By now, I'd formed and rebuilt teams at a few companies and felt well-equipped to do the same. Famous last words.

I was excited about the opportunity, but I didn't even take a moment to pause and ask if I wanted to take this position or if it would be right for me. After all, the phone rang, and that had to be God, right? I didn't have another option, did I?

Still navigating the divorce and being in a toxic dating relationship had me pretty shaken, but this job was something I could do. It was something I could control. Somehow, the conqueror mindset and standing in the face of fear had faded, and I let the nagging thought that I wouldn't be able to find something else take over. Just like that, I dove right in.

I wish I'd paused and reflected on questions like, *How will this role serve me? What is the environment? What are the organization's financial standings? What are the financial expectations? How will my success be measured? Do other executives in the organization respect and see purpose in this role?*

Instead, I jumped into rebuilding another company, transforming its operations, and navigating toxic workplace dynamics.

The lack of the "Power of the Pause" led to a tumultuous journey. If you haven't heard of this practice before, it's an intentional act of pausing—whether in conversation, decision-making, or personal reflection—to create space to gain clarity. I've seen this be instrumental in my leadership roles over the years, giving me time to frame more thoughtful responses and reduce any immediate impulse decisions. Especially when other stress-inducing factors are taking place around me or in my life. I didn't pause, and I stepped into another challenging season.

Not to say that I didn't learn from every experience, or meet and work with some fantastic people. However, over five years, I navigated broken communication channels and processes, stood my ground as I was cursed out in hallways, sat in executive meetings where I had to fight for a dribble of respect for my ideas and voice to be heard, taken on and achieved growth goals only to be told each time that we didn't quite make it and my bonus wouldn't be awarded. And then the final blow: learning that my trusted teammate and friend had worked for over a year to undermine me to my boss, plotting behind the scenes to take my position. Hearing what had transpired was painful, even though God had been trying to warn me through my gut instincts that this was coming.

I'll never forget that day. I shook my boss's hand and thanked them for the opportunity. I gathered my things, walked down the hall I'd walked for years, took that last trip down the elevator, and out the front door. Shock. Anger. And then—relief.

Stepping outside that building for the last time, the sun hit my face like a warm embrace. "Thank you, God," I whispered. I had been moved out of something that no longer served me.

Remember that Proverb, "Many are the plans in a person's heart, but the Lord's will prevails." I was living it. Reflecting on the drive home, I realized I had accomplished exactly what I was assigned and more. The company was now a stand-alone agency serving specific markets, new talented team members were in place, my work focus led to new processes, service offerings, and pricing structures, and I'd repaired broken relationships. I leveled up with renewed courage, resiliency, perseverance, hope, peace, and healthy pride.

A severance check gave me time to reflect. That would have been the best time to start my own business, but it had never really been in my heart to do that. Instead, I returned to old habits and started looking for another job, updating my resume, and networking. Instead of immediately job-hunting, I should have asked:

What do I truly want? Should I start my own business? What are my strengths? Who can mentor me?

But fear took over. An old colleague, now a CEO, offered me a role. I lept again.

During that time, I also launched a faith-based podcast with a dear friend called *Zvedá: She Rises to Impact Generations*, where we coached young women in various areas of their career journey. Stepping out to meet new people and try new things lit a spark deep inside. I loved building cultures and began to see how much I loved leading my own thing. Leaning into the "Power of the Pause" would've been an excellent step for me at this point. Reflecting through questions like the following may have gotten me to business ownership faster:

Where am I financially? How many months do I have to pay for my needs? Do I need an immediate position? Is this the time to outline a plan to start my own business? What are my top strengths and areas of expertise? How can I sell that? Do I need a mentor or coach to guide me?

But instead, I let that fear well up and take over, again. During that year of hustling to find a job, I was hired to begin a specific project for one of my past clients. She was a colleague of over fifteen years and a friend of mine. Little did I know, but she was searching for someone with operational skills that matched my exact makeup. We had joked over the years that I would work for her one day. I was one of the founding clients of her then-new business. Things were about to come full circle.

I shared my resume with her and asked her to pass it along to her board in case they had any connections. Until then, the interview process had not landed me that next fantastic gig. As her board reviewed it, someone pointed out that I had the skills she sought. Before the end of that year, she offered me a position as Chief Operating Officer, and I stepped into a new year with a new position. I was so excited! I leveled up.

Once again, I didn't pause or ask the right questions. Not that it would have changed my decision, but in reflection, I realized that asking key questions could have helped inform my choice and strengthened my role as a new team member and employee.

What are your goals for this position? How will my success be measured? What is the financial standing of the organization? What is the sales process? Where do you want to be as an owner in three to five years? Where do you want the business to be in three to five years? What is your vision for what I am to accomplish in this role?

She outlined the task of establishing processes across the organization and leading the client account team. I accepted the position and was off to the races.

Then, the pandemic hit. No leader was prepared for this experience. Within a few months of my start date, we closed the physical office space and transitioned our team from full-time in-office employees to remote employees. Thankfully, we already had processes and tools to make that transition more manageable, but we faced unknowns, business shifts, and the challenge of strengthening our culture.

This is where I learned that executive leadership can play a massive role in supporting an owner, though I didn't realize it then. Business owners will tell you, "It's lonely at the top," which can be very accurate. In an executive intrapreneurship role, you can dig in and almost force your way into the owner's thought processes, to be a support system and offer perspectives. I also learned that owners must ask for help. It may feel lonely, but we don't have to do it alone. Many women leaders want to appear to have everything figured out to protect the team from worry, and I've been in that exact situation.

But the truth is, no one has it all figured out. In times of uncertainty or significant change, whether good or challenging, pausing is essential.

I've now had to face this as a business owner. These questions have helped me navigate challenges and use my trusted team members and advisors to give me insights and support. It doesn't mean that I act on every idea, but it does provide new perspectives. Looking back, I wish we had worked through some of these questions together, not just for the organization but for my own leadership growth.

Key practices like a SWOT (Strengths, Weaknesses, Opportunities, Threats) analysis with an added clear action plan based on realistic goals would have helped. Asking questions such as:

What are our strengths? What are our weaknesses? What opportunities does this situation present? What threats do we face? Where do we need support? What are our gaps? How are we doing personally? Are we minding the crucial aspects of ourselves (mental and physical health)? Do we need to consider pivoting? What should the team structure be? Where do we need to cut costs to prepare for the future? What are the financial implications?

As top performers, we often try to hide our true feelings about challenges and hesitate to ask for help, not because we fear failure but because we care too much about what others think. What will "they" say? Oh, that proverbial "they". I hesitated to ask certain things because I felt it wasn't my place.

For so long, I was consumed by the weight of others' opinions—constantly seeking validation, fearing judgment, and second-guessing my own instincts. But those limiting mindsets began to shift when I started trusting myself and shifting my focus to faith.

Instead of looking for outward approval, I turned inward and upward, grounding myself in the truth that my worth, talents, and strengths weren't defined by others' perceptions. I still have empathy for what others may feel, but I no longer let it dictate my choices. By implementing daily morning quiet times to focus on truth from scripture and listening to mindset-shifting leaders, I have found the freedom to live authentically and unapologetically.

It wasn't an easy process, and those little nasty limiting beliefs can creep up, but I've gained practices to focus on the thoughts and feelings and allow them to come (thank you to my coach, Jasen Edwards). Then to take a moment and dig a bit deeper to see where those thoughts and feelings are originating from, to get to the real root of the fear or limiting belief.

I then read the promises that I know are for my life that I've gathered and saved from scriptures over the years, like my key life verse, Isaiah 54. Things that are uplifting and encouraging to reset my mind on topics like abundant provision and hopeful expectation.

I look back at my gratitude journals to review all of the blessings that I have received, and I read them out loud. There is a powerful thing that happens when we state positive things about our life out loud. Our brains record it as truth, and over time, we begin walking in that truth. I also make a list of affirmations of where I desire to be in my life, and then record a voice memo and play it back on my walks.

Statements like, you are greatly favored and highly blessed, you are confident, brave, and a conqueror, you have talents that others need to be encouraged and to be successful in their work and lives, everything you touch today will be a success, and so on. I've also learned not to sit alone with the doubts and fears, but to seek help, not for validation, but for insights that will strengthen my decisions.

Asking for help and bringing up complex topics that challenge the status quo is the only way to break through obstacles, and many times, it offers a perspective that can take the business in an entirely new direction. All of these practices led to an encouraged and positive mindset, which affected my leadership in so many ways.

Another key lesson I learned, particularly during the pandemic, was the importance of assessing situations but making decisions faster. Speed is key to success.

Perfectionism is the killer of business growth. You may have heard the phrases "fail fast" and, "Done is better than perfect." They couldn't be more accurate. The key is to be thoughtful with a plan, but get to the launch quickly. Create, launch, test, and adjust. If something isn't working, reassess, tweak, and relaunch.

I used to say I had a long rope when addressing performance issues, slow-moving launches, or lagging sales. I thought it was a strength, but it wasn't. True strength is creating clarity around goals and expectations. When things aren't aligning, I've learned to trust my gut and make a change. Will people always agree? No. Will you always be liked? Probably not. However, a team depends on decisive leadership, whether they recognize it at the time or not.

We made it through the pandemic. We redefined success overnight. It was a masterclass in crisis leadership.

However, we again experienced tough times. From slow sales and client loss to staff changes, we were forced to examine ourselves as a business, which was an excellent opportunity to pivot.

That year, we narrowed our offerings to focus on what we did best and the clients we desired to work with. The narrowing would provide a foundation of focus for the business, allow our team to work in the areas they were most skilled, allow us to own thought leadership in a specific industry, and get back to serving clients, working to impact our communities. We didn't just flip a switch and start, but I spent time talking to other business owners who had done the same thing and was encouraged that we could make this work.

Then, as the owner and I sat at a coffee shop, I received an unexpected offer, "Would you be interested in buying the business?"

What?

The Big Decision

Fear gripped me, and a new set of questions permeated my mind.

Could I afford it? Was I capable? What if I failed?

Inside, my mind was racing. It was like the last too many years to count, and everything came flooding back. That sitting at the red light in the rain, looking in the rearview mirror moment. Here I was again. Sitting. Frozen. Shocked. Scared.

How would this even be possible? I didn't have the cash to write a big check. Was this the right opportunity for me? What the actual hell? What about my plan? [Enter another LOL moment.] I think I responded with something like, "Oh wow. I'm honored. I'll have to think about that."

If you haven't caught it, all along my journey, when I wasn't moving, God moved things for me. From country girl to big city, from entry-level positions and job loss to a CEO seat.

All along, He's been guiding me toward owning my own business and creating something that is mine. That would lead me down a path to my purpose. With every challenge, change, and what would seem a setback, it was preparation. I was leveling up all along the way.

The next few months of this process would be HARD. There were many things I wasn't prepared to face, but navigating and learning this process has positioned me to now help others in a similar position. To help other women considering business ownership from the position of intrepreneur. The big plus for me was that I was stepping into owning something established with a good brand reputation and a foundation I had helped build over my five-year tenure. This set the stage for me to focus on revenue growth vs. repair. My situation was also unique in that I had worked with our founder for years as a client before joining as a team member. Then, I worked on the business operationally before stepping in as owner.

The biggest hurdle I had to jump over was coming to terms with the decision. You see, I planned to work FOR someone and continue to be a strong intrepreneur, and it was hard to have the owner tell me that she desired to move on. After all, we were building together, weren't we?

One of the key things I needed to do was grieve. I wanted to say goodbye to the plan I thought I was working toward. I wanted to let go of what I thought my job and role would be and clean the slate to prepare my heart and mind to carry out something new. I also had to recognize that everyone has the right to their journey. If the founder wanted to try something new that would inspire her and give her life, that was just as important as my wanting to achieve what I desired for my life.

I took my advice this time and used the "Power of the Pause."

I journaled. Prayed. I asked hard questions. Let go of my old plan and stepped into the decision to buy the business.

I just didn't want to see all of the hard work come to an end, like so many years invested from various team members and the last five from me. There were so many opportunities yet to be tapped into, and I felt a fire in my gut to bring them to life.

The valuation process began. I consulted legal counsel, financial advisors, and mentors. Although the negotiations were emotional, I remained firm.

Finally, I lept. I became a business owner.

Today, I own Bloom Communications, a company dedicated to helping mission-driven organizations thrive with new offerings created to serve leaders and businesses in new ways including organizational strategic planning, marketing strategies that drive awareness and engagement, for nonprofits donor stewardship and fundraising strategies and plans, and launching supportive digital tools like ebooks and workshops, plus stepping into my passion of leadership coaching for women on the climb. Every lesson, every setback, every moment of rushing forward without reflection led me here. But now, I move forward differently.

Bloom Communications was founded to create change in our communities by working with nonprofit organizations and mission-driven companies that truly care about doing the hard work to solve issues and needs in the areas in which we live, work, and play. It was founded to provide fun and engaging careers for great people, provide for families, and work with amazing clients. My vision is to keep this amazing founding mission alive and continue to add to the business, offering key programs, workshops, and services that expand organizational awareness, ultimately to ensure businesses and leaders are growing.

My journey unfolded with triumphs, painful lessons, and moments that felt like hell on Earth. Every experience shaped me into the leader I am today. But I've learned that leveling up isn't just about pushing forward. It requires pausing to reflect—looking in the rearview mirror, assessing past failures and successes, and making informed choices for the road ahead.

Looking back, I see how each job, hardship, and unexpected twist was a step toward something more significant. But back then, I didn't pause to consider the bigger picture. I moved, hustled, and leaped before I looked. Each transition was another chance to prove myself, keep the momentum going, and push forward.

I know now that I should have taken a breath before each leap and asked the hard questions: *What is this next step really offering me? Will it serve my strengths? What do I need from this role beyond a paycheck? Will this work environment support my growth? How will my team thrive? And how will I thrive?*

Now, I pause. I ask the right questions and step on the gas with intention when the light turns green.

The fear still lingers, but I move forward anyway. I am discovering what I want my business to be, the clients I want to serve, and the legacy I want to build.

Failures will come. I will fail fast and learn faster. However, I will keep my eyes on the mission: Provide for my team, family, and community.

So, where are you right now? Are you moving so fast that you haven't stopped to reflect? Are you at a red light, wondering what's next? If so, take a breath. Look in the rearview mirror. See how far you've come. Celebrate every milestone—even the trials.

Then, like me, look up. The light just turned green.

Step on the gas. Let's go.

JAMIE MATUSEK

Jamie Matusek is the Owner and CEO of Bloom Communications. Described as the Chief Encouragement Officer, Jamie is a master of navigating life's most challenging transitions—motherhood, divorce, layoffs, promotions, or new ventures. Each of these experiences has shaped her into the coach and entrepreneur she is today.

With her coaching certification and a personal mission rooted in empowering other women, Jamie is dedicated to helping women step boldly into their next chapter. She focuses on vital topics such as healing mindsets, overcoming fear, setting and achieving meaningful goals, and cultivating joy even amid life's trials.

With twenty-nine years of experience spanning operations, team and culture development, and brand growth through integrated marketing strategies, Jamie is uniquely equipped to guide others through change.

As the owner of Bloom Communications, she prioritizes fostering a strong team culture, streamlined processes, leadership development, and impactful employee training. Jamie also oversees the development of innovative client brand strategies, bringing the same passion to her business as she does to her personal mission.

Those who know Jamie describe her as an encourager, an overcomer, and someone who inspires with her faith, vision, and unwavering belief in others. Through her work, Jamie aims to help women discover their true passions and strengths, equipping them to thrive individually and collectively in ways that make a lasting impact.

Instagram: @jamietheceo
LinkedIn: jamiematusek

9

THE OTHER SIDE OF COMFORT

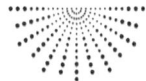

BY ABIGAIL SEYMOUR

Of all the things that stick in my mind from that day, the one I remember the most is the tissue box. It was a plain white box, the kind that wasn't intended to soothe with pretty drawings, just dispense. The tissue sticking out at the top was fluffed just so.

The box was in the middle of a small beige conference table in a windowless room, soft indirect lighting in one corner, and a framed abstract drawing of a vaginal-looking flower hung between the lamp and the door. I heard a soft knock and a man in a lab coat entered, his lips pursed, head down.

I went to this suite of offices a few days before, and was still smarting on my right side from the six-inch needle that had biopsied a lump I had found but was quite sure was "nothing," since eight out of ten of breast lumps are benign cysts. I didn't have time to fret about the outcome, let alone face whatever it might mean if the results were bad.

I had just gotten to the other side of one the riskiest and perhaps dumbest moves of my life: A complete career change. Not just a pivot, but a catapult from one side of the working world to another, like starting out life as a skateboard and deciding to become a racecar. They both have wheels, but that's about all they have in common.

I have had lots of 9-5 jobs over the years, none of which felt right. I always felt trapped. I even tried to jazz up the kinds of places I worked, changing it up from a sleek, uber-corporate management consulting firm where I was a temp just after college and seeking out a vibrant, bright-colored theatrical producer's office, my small desk being literally above the cavernous stage below, where I could hear the orchestra on Wednesday matinee days.

My desire to escape was so strong even then that I chucked a traditional job for living abroad and teaching English to professionals, popping into their drab, corporate offices for an hour or two and then gratefully leaving to be back out in the blazing sunlight before my next gig. But my ambition was always telling me that simply running from place to place was only a temporary fix for my restlessness.

After three years abroad in Europe, I came back to the U.S., having had enough of threadbare living to actually wish again for the hum-drum stability of a nine-to-five job. I just wanted to unpack my homemade lunch from an insulated lunchbox and sit quietly somewhere to gather my thoughts. I did that for a few years, but without any real direction, and a permanent conversion back to a nine-to-five was not going to work, and before long, I was cooking up yet another scheme to become my own boss.

My college degree was in visual arts, and I was a moody, creative mimic of the work of photographers like Diane Arbus and Henri Cartier-Bresson. When I took inventory of my skills, photography seemed like an obvious one to use for making a living. So I set my sights on becoming a high-end family photographer—and I did it.

I traveled to Las Vegas, Florida, New York, and all around North Carolina to capture the stories of families and lovers beginning their lives together. I built a six-figure business over ten years, had two children in the middle of it, and taught workshops to other professionals on how to grow their businesses.

But years of being away from home every Saturday night, driving home after midnight with tired eyes and toddlers at home took a toll on me. I remember distinctly the moment a young woman showed me a photo of the dress she had picked out, and I couldn't see it without putting on my reading glasses.

I was in my mid-forties by then, closer in age to her mom than I was to her. It was 2008 and the ATM machine of home equity and stock market wealth to pay for lavish weddings (and photographers) dried up overnight. I didn't want to face the truth, but I had just spent a decade climbing the entrepreneurial ladder only to find that it was leaning against the wrong wall. I couldn't stop thinking about the fact that all I had done was create a job for myself that didn't pay me enough, and to which I felt chained.

Again.

In the past, when I had come to the end of a work chapter, it was an uncomfortable conversation with a supervisor that lasted maybe thirty minutes. And then I was on my way out the door, never to look back. But ending this work chapter, that of winding up my own business, was a gut-wrenching, months-long dismantling of what felt like my very identity. I had never been the last one in the building who turns off the lights for the last time, the one who takes a box-cutter blade to peel the vinyl letters with my own name and logo from the front door.

I didn't have a plan, I just wanted *out* of being the boss by that point. I wanted to be a W-2 employee again, something I hadn't been for nine years. As long as I didn't ever have to be the one signing the checks, if I could just wave hello in the mornings, sit at a desk that I didn't buy, check a computer for messages on an email server I didn't have to set up, I would be fine.

It took me exactly three days of working for someone else as her assistant in a therapy practice, with a camera in the ceiling above me live-streaming my every move, having to write down all the things I had accomplished that day and to be accused of "reading" her files (which was, in fact, part of my job description) to cure me of that temptation to return to that old lover again.

But whatever I took on as my next venture had to be sustainable. It had to be something I could do until I was an old woman, something that valued wisdom, maturity, experience, and was never boring.

I was going to become a lawyer.

By the time I was sitting in that doctor's office anteroom, I had almost done it. I had survived three years of law school, graduated just after my 50th birthday, gotten the highest grade in my legal writing class, interned at local non-profit and government agencies, and had taken the dreaded bar exam.

My identity as a wedding professional and the memory of shutting my business down had been almost completely erased. I had managed to turn into a racecar. Well, at least I was no longer a skateboard.

The results from the NC Bar Exam, the last hill I needed to climb into this new life, would be coming any day now, I didn't have the bandwidth to be sideswiped by anything, let alone have a crowbar jammed into the spokes of my wheels:

"You have breast cancer."

The pursed-lip radiologist didn't actually need to say those words, because the only thing he was carrying when he entered the room was a gift bag with a pink ribbon on the side.

I didn't take a tissue, I didn't move, I just stared at the pink ribbon while he said words I couldn't hear and removed items from the bag: A book called "The Breast Cancer Survival Manual", a list of local resources and hotlines, a knitted pink scarf, and an appointment card for my date with the cancer center next week. It took all my strength not to hurl the tissue box and everything in that bag right at his head.

When I got back to my apartment, the one I had just moved into after separating from my husband of twenty years, I saw a lone envelope poking out of the mailbox next to the front door. My bar exam results. Surely this day couldn't get much worse.

"We regret to inform you..." was all I needed to see.

In a strange way, I was relieved, since I secretly wanted someone to confirm for me that what I was undertaking was irresponsible. Now I could easily explain, if anyone asked, that unfortunately, I did not pass the bar, but since I was battling cancer, it was not of concern to me anymore.

I spent the next six months learning new phrases like *in situ*, sentinel lymph nodes, aromatase inhibitors, and oligometastasis.

As I was well enough after my surgery, I looked for a job, with increasing lack of success. I did some remote assistant work for an estates attorney, and answered phones for a commercial cleaning company. I taught swim lessons to five-year-olds at the YMCA. I grieved.

I was looking for confirmation that I didn't need to keep trying, that the Universe had told me that my body couldn't handle the stress of studying for yet another 200 hours and sitting for a twelve-hour exam.

My children were in fourth and fifth grade at the time, learning all about perseverance and courage in the brightly colored biographies of historical figures. There weren't any books about people who tried once, failed, and then said, "I'm done."

"Everything you want is on the other side of comfort." A therapist told me when I sidled up to the idea of maybe it was okay for me to stop trying.

The only time I think about that awful year now is when I undress for bed and shrug off my bra, with one side a silicone prosthesis with the weight and heft of a chicken cutlet. The flat scar that goes across my right side has faded almost completely. There is a prevailing myth that Amazon women warriors would hack off their own right breast to make it easier to fire arrows at their enemies. Instead of moping about how I can't wear a low-cut dress (something I never did anyway) I am proud of my lopsided, warrior silhouette.

I finally did pass the bar exam, even though it took two more tries, 600 more hours of studying, and twenty-four hours of test-taking over the course of eighteen months. I was waging a battle against my own stubbornness as much as against microscopic cells trying to kill me. I was just going to keep taking the exam until I passed it, or died.

I went to work for a law firm for a year, showing up at 8:30 a.m. as required, labeling my food in the breakroom fridge, and signing cards for people's birthdays. My paycheck was direct-deposited reliably, and I had my own windowless office.

The kind of law I was attracted to is known as direct service, representing everyday people in their struggles with a marriage that has collapsed, conflict with the other parent of their kids, a family dispute over inheritance, speeding ticket, immigration help, or "kitchen table law."

Nothing is more sacred to me than that quiet conversation where a complete stranger wants to, needs to, tell me something that they really haven't told anyone. I couldn't help but see a parallel to the intimacy I was privileged to have with my photography clients a decade before, a front row seat to their families as they got ready for a wedding, their babies during the first year of life. I wanted to be able to take my time with them, send them home with a book that might help, send a card to follow up, check in on them. But I had a full schedule of other client meetings and court, and no time to give that personal touch.

After a few months, I began thinking of ideas to pitch to the owners, ways of expanding marketing efforts and client care, plus maybe a way to spruce up the logo and upgrade the internal case management systems. I didn't realize that those are not employee thoughts, those are entrepreneur thoughts, and I was, in fact, designing my future law firm.

I gave notice after a year, and by then, I had already recorded the outgoing message for the law firm that existed only in my mind. I envisioned a place with warm decor, couches, office dogs, windows, and, someday, more than one person there. When I recorded that outgoing message, "You have reached Camino Law..." I sat on my living room floor and played a recording in the background called "Busy Office Sounds" from YouTube —phones ringing, people talking, doors opening and closing.

It sounded like we were already busy and successful, and I had only a logo and a shared office space in a corporate office park near my house. I didn't have any clients, no website, and a three-month commitment to an expensive pay-per-lead company that promised cases.

My first client was a woman who had recently gotten out of prison for heroin trafficking and whose daughter was in the custody of her great-aunt.

"The lady at the courthouse office told me I could just transfer custody," she told me during our consultation.

It took five years of wrangling and court dates canceled during Covid lockdown and multiple clean drug tests and motions, but she got her daughter back. She taught me how to be a lawyer and advocate more than anyone.

When I watch time-lapse videos of people cleaning their houses, or creating a piece of artwork, or a flower changing from bud to bursting, it happens so seamlessly and fast. I built my business slowly, but nobody watches the slow-motion videos of the flower growing.

I knew from my earlier experience as a business owner whose operations shut down, that I hadn't had any systems. So, I read *The E-Myth,* by Michael E. Gerber, which is considered a mandatory read for anyone who wants to have more than one person in their enterprise. The book teaches you how to create a three-ring binder of sorts with instructions on how you do everything so that you can hand it off to someone else. I didn't yet have anyone to hand it off to, but I started writing it just the same.

In both the business-building and lawyer-learning communities, I never encountered anything but generosity. Attorneys would take my calls, answer my questions, and send me samples of pleadings I needed to use as my templates. I joined online groups of solo practitioners and people wanting to "hang a shingle." And one by one, I represented clients. I learned their stories, their fears, their pain points, and extended my genuine interest in them and in solving their problems.

The only way I could measure whether I was doing any of it correctly was by how much the phone rang. I needed help and hired my first employee, followed by hiring someone to be her assistant. The three-ring binder got added to, pages crossed through, and rewritten as we grew.

We had a little birthday party for the business when it turned two years old. We moved into a converted Victorian-style house near my city's downtown area and put up a sign out front. We installed a little free library, and one of the rooms in the building became a fully-equipped playroom for the children of clients. (I once visited a family law firm with a sign in the lobby that said, "No children allowed," which seemed exceptionally tone-deaf. I vowed to do just the opposite someday.)

I applied to and was accepted into a program sponsored by Goldman Sachs called 10,000 Small Businesses, a way to bolster the economy through smaller entities around the country.

One of the first questions we were asked to address was "What is your exit plan?"

This is a shocking question to someone who has just had business cards printed, but it is indeed part of the boat-burning process. If you don't know where you are going, you are sure to get there.

If I burned the boat of my old life, I am now navigating the waves in a dinghy hammered together with the driftwood from what is left over. But it's floating, and it is mine.

Just yesterday, in one of the two buildings that my firm and its nine women employees now occupy (we outgrew the original house and expanded into the one next door), I sat across from a client to advise her on her rights and options as she winds up her twenty-four-year marriage to a husband whose infidelity broke her heart and destroyed the life they had together. As we talked more, she confided that her marriage had fallen apart a few years ago when she was diagnosed with breast cancer.

I reached across the table to take her hands in mine. Then she stood up and lifted her shirt to show her scar, so I did the same. We hugged. We had both been transformed by things out of our control, shirked off our old lives, and had made it to the other side.

There is a tissue box in that office, but ours is in a whimsical, decorative box, one that looks like a small house, the tissue coming out of the "chimney." A little saying is framed on the wall near where clients sit which reads, "A lot of things change, but not the fact that I'm a motherfucking goddess."

ABIGAIL C. SEYMOUR

Abigail Seymour is the founder and CEO of Camino Law, an all-female law firm in Greensboro, North Carolina, where she and four other attorneys focus their practice on family law, including surrogacy and grandparent custody as well as family-based immigration, including VAWA and SIJS.

A second-career attorney, Abigail went to law school at forty-seven after a career as a photographer and journalist. She lived in Spain after college and speaks fluent Spanish. Abigail has been a speaker and podcast guest on the topic of reinvention, second careers, and healthy co-parenting.

Abigail is a Goldman Sachs 10,000 Small Businesses scholar and the recipient of an Empowering Women award from NC Lawyers Weekly for her innovative approach to creating a non-traditional and mom-friendly law firm culture.

She received her Bachelor's (BA) from New York

University's Tisch School of the Arts, and her Juris Doctor (JD) from Elon University School of Law.

Abigail is also a bestselling author for her co-authored book called *Law Moms: Juggling Motherhood, Ambition & Personal Fulfillment.*

Connect with Abigail:

Facebook: https://www.facebook.com/abigail.seymour
Instagram: @abigail_c_seymour
TikTok: @abogada_abigail

OUR NON-PROFIT PARTNERS

Spread the love!

All proceeds from our multi-author books are donated to a nonprofit organization making a meaningful difference in the lives of women or children in Austin, Texas, where Sulit Press is headquartered.

By purchasing this book, you're not only supporting the voices and stories of the women who contributed— you're also helping fund real change in the local community.

We periodically select new nonprofit partners to ensure that the impact of each book continues to reach where it's needed most.

To learn more about our current partner organization, please visit our website at www.sulitpress.com.

Ready to fast-track your publishing career, increase your visibility, or boost your business?

If this book is in your hands, chances are you've got something powerful to say, too.

At Sulit Press, we help women write just one chapter that opens doors—whether that's to new clients, speaking gigs, media features, or simply the joy of finally being published.

By contributing to a Multi-Author Book, you'll gain:

- A clear and supported path to becoming a published author
- Visibility for your work, business, or message
- A powerful network of fellow authors and creatives

This is for you if:

☑ You're passionate about what you do and ready to share it

☑ You're committed to showing up and doing your best work

☑ You're excited to be part of something bigger

Ready to explore what's possible?

Visit sulitpress.com to learn how you can get published, join a powerful community, and grow your visibility.